Think & Grow You:

How to Get Out of Your Own Way and

Level up Your Life

By: Chris Felton

Published 2023

Paperback Print ISBN: 978-1-66640-018-2
Ebook ISBN: 978-1-66640-020-5
Hardcover ISBN: 978-1-66640-019-9

Get the Think & Grow You Bonus Bundle

Visit www.chrisfelton.me/book/bookbonuses to get access to Chris Felton's Think & Grow You bonus bundle.

Tap into Chris' thoughts, actions, and strategies that will change your life forever, including:

- ➤ Printable PDF book of Think & Grow You quotes
- ➤ Printable PDF book of Think & Grow You resources
- ➤ Printable PDF book of The Quotable Chris Felton
- ➤ Printable PDF book of Think & Grow You action steps, including journaling space to complete each action step
- ➤ Exclusive content with Chris
- ➤ Access to all of Chris' social media channels

Prologue

Chris' life was unraveling, and his back was against the wall. He was staring down an impossible financial situation. Multiple six figures of credit card debt and negative monthly cashflow which contributed to a severely strained marriage. Entering the great recession as a financial services entrepreneur created more challenges. His little boys lived across the country and due to the financial constraints, he couldn't see them. "I'm a bad dad" kept swirling in his mind and he felt guilt for letting them down. He couldn't work any harder. It seemed like no matter what he did, nothing changed. He was STUCK! Stuck in every area of this life.

After a tumultuous fight with his wife, he had an awakening. Wherever he had a problem, he was always there. He was the common denominator to all his problems. He created the whole mess. It wasn't easy, but he took complete responsibility and realized he needed to change. That's what he did. He fully committed to growing and changing. It wasn't overnight, but eventually as he changed internally the outside world changed.

Think & Grow You is about this journey, which will teach you the following:

- How to get out of your own way. Doing the internal work helps us recognize our self-sabotaging tendencies that keep us stuck.
- How to shift, which is thinking and doing things differently to create better results.

- How to improve our relationships. Everything we want in life will come from and through people. Relationships are the key to a happy life and Chris shares his significant lessons that changed everything.
- How to gameplan and execute. Correct thinking is paramount, but we must also take action and execute a game plan whether we feel we're ready or not. Chris shares the key concepts that caused a quantum leap in his results.
- To have our dreams come true, we must know what we want and why. Chris shares how he created the necessary focus that manifested his dream life.

BE WILLING TO CHANGE.
DO THE WORK.
IT'S WORTH IT!!

Foreword

By Steve Siebold
Speaker, Author, Entrepreneur, and Business Coach

Chris Felton is fearless!

Not in the sense of charging into burning buildings but in revealing his darkest moments. This book is about the psychological dissection of a man that felt like a failure.

Recruited out of college by the world's most prestigious accounting firm, Felton worked hard to climb the corporate ladder. Yet, in his mind, it wasn't enough. Stressed out, overworked, and unhappy, he longed for a better life.

As the saying goes, be careful what you wish for. Making the leap from corporate America to entrepreneur, Chris jumped out of the frying pan into the proverbial fire. He was thrust into a business he didn't understand, while tragically, his personal life was falling apart.

Think and Grow You is Chris Felton's journey from a burned-out employee to a world-class entrepreneur. But not to worry---this isn't a tome full of positive thinking platitudes. Instead, this book is written in blood by a man that failed over and again…yet refused to quit. It's a playbook for moving from failure to success, personally and professionally, accompanied by the author's heart-wrenching events along the way.

I love this book because it brilliantly describes the kick-and-scratch story of success. It's winning ugly while being unapologetic.

Chris Felton's climb is not a get-rich-quick formula. Many have amassed faster fortunes. The beauty of this book is the grind, pain, and payoff of a man that couldn't be stopped.

Read this book carefully and put Felton's proven strategies into action. You'll be glad you did.

Steve Siebold
President
International Personal Development Association

Praise for Think & Grow You

"Chris Felton shares his fears, failures, and deep thoughts to help people realize they're not alone. It's real and relatable, with strategies to help people get unstuck and move forward. You'll be inspired to change your life.

Marshall Faulk - Pro Football Hall of Fame running back, entrepreneur & speaker

"This book made me cringe. It's written in blood. Chris Felton fearlessly exposes his darkest hours as a man seeking self-redemption. I couldn't put it down."

Steve Siebold - President, International Personal Development Association

"This book is jam-packed with some of the best personal development stories I've ever heard. It's a great read for anyone who wants to grow"

Dawn Andrews – President, Georgia Speaker's Bureau

"Think & Grow You is one of the most authentic, insightful, and relatable books that I've ever read. Chris' courage to share his personal struggles, and how he was able transform his life is admirable. These life changing lessons will benefit everyone. I found myself thanking Chris with every page I read. It has helped me become a better version of myself. It will do the same for you as well."

Jay Maymi - Founder & CEO, Survive to Thrive Enterprises

"The book you hold in your hands is full of real-world wisdom and advice. Chris writes like he speaks – full of passion and conviction. Take it to heart. Learn from it. Put it into practice. You won't regret it!"

Gwen Hartzler – Financial Advisor, entrepreneur, and author of Would You Follow You?

"This is a book for the advanced personal growth student, brand new goal strategist, or to set yourself back on track! Chris shares applicable (and relevant) take aways for both professional and personal development. Chris is a person who has continuously walked the walk and I read this book thinking the World now gets the cliff note version of thousands of hours of his training. A must read for any stage of development you are in."

Denise Lund – CEO, Find Neutral

"In the world of personal development, we often hear that life happens for us, not to us. But Think & Grow You, the new book from Chris Felton, turns that platitude on its head. Felton teaches us to stop being passive in the first place! Rather, he shows us how to be intentional and get out there and create the lives of our dreams regardless of what's happening around us."

Mark Hardcastle - Airline captain, speaker, trainer, and author of The Symphony of Your Life: Restoring Harmony When Your World Is Out of Tune

Introduction

We are either growing or dying.

Author Jeff Shore stated, "A life spent seeking comfort results in an entirely uncomfortable existence." If we aren't open to change, our lives don't change, and we remain stuck.

Often, instead of growing ourselves, we look to fix the outside. We rearrange the furniture on the deck of the Titanic. We believe that we will finally be good once the external factors are fixed. People, money, business, success; it's an endless search that results in fatigue and dissatisfaction. I know this story well and lived it for years. With my back against the wall, I finally realized that something had to change, and it was me.

I went all in on my commitment to grow and develop. If I hadn't, I was going to lose big. My marriage, finances, business, and the life that I knew. The price was too high. I was delusional to expect that the same person who made the mess would fix it. I had to grow.

This book is about that transformation. I'm not a guru, and I don't have it all figured out. Like you, I have problems, adversities, weaknesses, and strengths. I also fail and make mistakes. However, unlike most, I'm committed to continuous growth. My story proves that change is possible. I was a huge mess in several areas of my life, and I pray that my story provides you hope.

Don't rush through this book; there is no gold star for finishing. Slow down, think about the concepts, do the exercises, and apply. Don't get through the book; let the book get through you.

My growth has come from years of work. If you attempt to apply everything at once, you will not apply anything. So instead, pick an area and work on it until it becomes natural.

The book will be an ongoing resource. You'll come back, pick a topic, do an exercise, and shift. These aren't quick fixes, as it takes focus and persistence.

Author Mel Robbins says, "It doesn't work overnight, but it does work over time." If you stay on it, you will evolve and experience success. Most importantly, your success will positively impact those around you, so they know it's possible for them.

Table of Contents:

Foreword by Steve Siebold

Praise for Think & Grow You

Introduction

Pillar 1 - Get Out of Your Own Way

1.	Stop Worrying	3
2.	Be Done with It	5
3.	Stop Beating Yourself Up	9
4.	Quit Holding Yourself Back	11
5.	Quit Waiting	13
6.	Don't Settle	17
7.	You're Too Young to be Old	21
8.	Don't Wrestle With your Ego	25
9.	Quitter's Relief is a Lie, Don't Fall for It	29
10.	Don't Retreat	33

Pillar 2 – The Shift

11. Take 100% Responsibility	39
12. Draw a Line in the Sand	41
13. You Deserve It	43
14. Get Emotional	47
15. Get Aligned	49
16. What if 'Up'?	53
17. Grow Spiritually	57
18. Trust Your Gut	61
19. Acknowledge Yourself	63
20. Trust, It's Going to Be Okay	67
21. Stop Resisting	71

22. Don't Label Things as Good or Bad   75

Pillar 3 – Relationships

23. Don't Be an Approval Addict   81
24. Forgive   85
25. Stop Controlling   87
26. Mind The Gap   91
27. Stay Together   93
28. Check Your Motives   97
29. Your Need to be Right Will Cost You Your Life   101
30. Stop Judging   105
31. Be a Spark   109
32. Keep Your Word   113
33. Be a Giver   117

Pillar 4 – The Game Plan

34. Know Your A & B   123
35. Get a Coach   125
36. Get it Together   129
37. Don't Eat the Elephant   133
38. Work Hard, But Don't Make Hard Work of It   137
39. It's a Project, Not a Problem   139
40. Grow Up, Be Accountable   143
41. You Can Change, Do the Work   147
42. Respect Money   151
43. Finish!   153

Pillar 5 – The Dream

44. Know What You Want and Focus on It   159

45. Know The Feeling You Want   163
46. Affirm What You Want   167
47. Hold The Image   169
48. Get Wealthy   173
49. You Can Do It   177
50. It's Worth It   181

Conclusion

Acknowledgments

Pillar 1

Get Out of Your Own Way

THINK&GROW YOU

1. Stop Worrying

The worst emotion is worry. Our ego traps us between past regrets and fear of the future. We often miss living life in the here and now. What we think about grows. Whether the object of your focus is good or bad, the significance grows while the thoughts you avoid fade. The more you worry, the more relevant those worries become. Worrying is a habit that provides a false sense of control. It never turns a situation into a positive outcome. Usually, we have no control or influence over the outcome.

Yet the more you think of good fortune, the more you will experience.

Quote: "When I look back on all these worries, I remember the story of the old man who said on his deathbed that he had a lot of trouble in his life, most of which had never happened." – Winston Churchill, Former British Prime Minister.

Resource: *How to Stop Worrying and Start Living* by Dale Carnegie

Action Step: Break your worry pattern by journaling on a current issue. Ask yourself the following questions:

1. What am I afraid of?
2. What is the worst thing that can happen?
3. If that happens, what will I do?
4. Lastly, tell yourself that 99% of what you worry about never happens. If needed, think back on initial worries, and confirm that the actual events weren't even close to what your mind

created. Focus on the next step you can take to resolve this. If it is outside your control, trust and let it go.

5. Note how you feel before and after this exercise.

During my divorce, I took a cruise to Alaska. The first day, I received a call from my stressed-out attorney. Things were not going well, and the financial negotiations of my divorce were daunting. I quickly absorbed her stress and doubt. I was staring down financial devastation, and terror set in. My head was spinning, and my chest tightened. The five-day trip had just begun, and I was headed to paradise and hell at the same time. I contemplated getting off the ship and flying home, but I refused to allow my ego to overrun me. However, the stress kept coming in waves, and the fear continued to mount.

The most beautiful stop was Sitka, Alaska. It was 60 degrees, and the views were stunning. I have a picture from that day, and the look on my face says it all. I was trapped in fear and worry.

When I got back to the boat, I decided that I was done being a victim. I went to the ship's theatre, armed with some great books and a pad of paper. I read, journaled, and pondered. After several hours, I realized that 99% of what I worry about never occurs. I concluded that it was a waste of time and let it go.

I had an amazing trip. Whenever my thoughts shifted back to my problems, I reminded myself to return to the present moment. It was a groundbreaking experience. I learned that I could control my thinking with some intention and focus.

2. Be Done with It!

Many of us are consumed by the thought of "one day, things will be better." It's the habit of forecasting the future while floundering in the present. The proverbial "line in the sand" moment never happens. Instead, overthinking, indecision, procrastination, excuses, and hesitation rule the day. Our problems appear larger than life, and we see no solution. Looking at the elephant, we can't figure out how to eat it in one bite. We doubt our ability to solve the problem.

This could manifest itself in starting a business, ending a bad relationship, or overcoming an addiction. We create the story that "once all these external conditions line up, I can move," or "once all the stop lights turn green, I can leave my house." We need someone else's opinion or insight before we can move. This keeps us stuck.

On the contrary, there is power in adopting the declaration of "I am done with this." Done with indecision, struggle, debt, etc. You can feel it in your heart. It's a powerful shift from desperation to determination. This moves you from an external to an internal locus of control. The result of this subtle shift in thinking is empowerment, self-reliance, and confidence.

Quote: "Sometimes you just have to be done, not mad, not upset. Just done." – Unknown.

Resource: *Feel the Fear and Do it Anyway* by Susan Jeffers, Ph.D.

Action Step: Journal:

1. What is one problem that has been lingering and taking up brain space?
2. What have you been telling yourself needs to happen externally to move?
3. Think and then write, "I am done with this."
4. What is the next step you can take to change your life?

During Christmas 2008, the trip to Atlanta to see my boys was extremely difficult. Our financial mess was getting worse. Our funds were limited, and my hopes of continuing to see my kids every 4-6 weeks were no longer feasible. This only fed my guilt. At ages 4 and 7, they were growing up without their Dad, and I was missing their events and activities.

"You're a bad Dad" was swirling around in my head, and I had evidence. I worried about how this would impact them; it was already a long-distance relationship. Observing my friends with their kids every day was painful.

I didn't see them in the summer of 2008. We couldn't afford it, Marlow, my wife, was strongly opposed to them visiting. She was right. I didn't know how to tell them there would be no summer visit, and I was riddled with guilt. The year before, I had to meet with clients to pay the bills during their summer visit. The trip didn't go well. I was with them physically but not mentally. Worry and fear dominated my mind. They could feel the tension and stress in our home.

It was the last day of my Christmas trip, and I had to head to the airport. Heartbroken, I told my kids, "I'm not sure when I'm going to see you again. Your Dad needs to work on some things and the financial situation is tight. It doesn't mean that I don't love you because I do. I'm going to get it figured out and I promise, I will make it up to you."

It was brutal; it was a year before I saw them again. However, driving to the airport, through tremendous tears, the decision was made. They were paying a heavy price, and so was I. The decision was finally made. I was done with this. And that was the day I started my trek toward financial prosperity. Today, the kids are thriving, and our relationship is stronger than ever.

3. Stop Beating Yourself Up

As children, we were programmed to believe that beating ourselves up psychologically was an effective strategy. If we criticized ourselves enough, things would eventually change.

Criticism came from parents, teachers, and coaches. Their well-intentioned berating became our internal disapproval. Often, they projected their own issues onto us. Either way, it didn't work.

This flawed premise promotes that being kind to ourselves is for losers. It makes us soft and lazy. Wrong! Hammering ourselves destroys self-confidence and lowers our energy. We anchor beliefs that convince us of our inferiority. It's difficult to achieve anything feeling this way.

A negative self-image creates negative results. Good or bad, life is experienced based on how we see ourselves.

Do we need to improve? Absolutely. Telling ourselves to improve is a positive. Without a relationship to results, we become delusional and fail. Just don't end the assessment with "you loser, you suck, etc." Look at results from discernment instead of judgment. Assess how to get better, course correct, and move forward.

Quote: "Beating yourself up is like trying to get out of a hole while digging it deeper." – Gail Lynne Goodwin, Author, Speaker, and Entrepreneur.

Resource: *What to Say When You Talk to Yourself* by Shad Helmstetter

Action Step: Journal about

1. What do you say when you talk to yourself?
2. What results does this create?
3. Who pays the price for you beating yourself up?
4. What issues does it create?
5. Is there any benefit?
6. Conclude that it isn't serving you and shift.
7. Select an affirmation or scripture to interrupt the pattern.
8. Say it until you feel emotional relief.
9. Resolve to pay attention to the conversation in your head.

In childhood, I was often reminded of my flaws. Beating myself up was ingrained, and it became a habit. Parents, teachers, and coaches believed being tough on us would create success. They thought we would be better prepared to overcome a difficult world.

Maybe it worked for some, but it had the opposite effect on me. I saw myself as inferior and was afraid of failure. I held myself back. Failing led to internal voices of negative judgment. Beating myself up didn't work. I had some success, but the negative judgment was painful. In adulthood, the constant hammer of self-doubt consumed me. It impacted everything. I was an overachiever, but the journey was arduous.

I was my own worst enemy, which created suffering for my loved ones and me. It was time to forgive and accept myself. I took control of my self-talk and became my biggest fan. My level of joy and happiness skyrocketed. My results improved while my life transformed.

4. Quit Holding Yourself Back

We often protect our self-esteem to avoid failure. The pain of past losses controls our decision-making so we avoid risk. We stick with jobs we hate because we're afraid of failing. We attribute losses to external events. We hesitate to act because we're unsure. We don't start the business. We don't speak up. We're not excited. Instead, we feel guilty and do just enough to get by. We overthink and don't ask for help.

It takes more energy to hold ourselves back than to launch. It's like holding a beach ball underwater: it's strenuous. If we keep holding ourselves back, we never get what we want. Take a step. Figure it out as you go. You are better than you think you are.

Quote: "Maybe you don't have to push yourself forward. Maybe you just have to stop holding yourself back." – Doe Zantamanta, Author.

Resource: *The Book of Est* by Luke Rhinehart

Action Step: Journal:

1. What's holding you back?
2. Make a list.
3. What does this create in your life?
4. What is your next step to move forward?
5. Pick one item on the list and work on it for the next 30+ days.

Early in my entrepreneurial journey, a mentor shared his first goal-setting step. He didn't initially dive into planning and setting goals. Instead, he asked himself, "What's holding me back?" He journaled for hours and created a big list. For months, he only focused on one or two items to change. Then he would go to the next thing. The more self-aware he became, the bigger the list grew.

He was growing exponentially and constantly improving. I wasn't. It sounded good, but I wasn't coachable.

I was struggling, and I didn't know why. It wasn't from a lack of effort. Something had to change. One Monday, I had eight client appointments scheduled. To make it financially, I needed all of them to close. They ALL canceled! Not rescheduled, CANCELED! Everyone disappeared. I wondered what I was going to do. My tendency was to medicate myself with cocktails. My gut told me to follow my mentor's advice.

I went to a quiet bookstore. I wrote, "What is holding me back?" at the top of my journal.

For five hours, I thought and wrote. It was a huge list: Hitting the snooze button, being unprepared, drinking too much, worrying, procrastination, and other deep issues. It was obvious. I had finally met the enemy, and it was me. I was running a marathon with a 20lb bowling ball attached to my ankle.

The exercise was freeing. It was the first time I was completely honest with myself. It wasn't about being perfect. It was about getting better and not beating myself up. I focused on the first thing on the list for a few months and then the next. I improved 5-7 items per year, and my whole world changed.

5. Quit Waiting

People look for external validation before committing. It sounds like, "Once this happens, then..." and it's an endless list. Waiting on a loved one to change before you are happy. Waiting to know more before launching a business. Waiting for the economy to change or for the right President. Waiting on their leader/boss for direction. Waiting for their team to take action before they do. Waiting to have more time. Waiting until their kids are grown. Waiting until they feel like it.

They live in Hopium, hoping things change externally while insisting on staying the same. We listen to the opinions of others vs. trusting our own. We live life wanting a guarantee before we commit. We only want to take safe risks. We allow others to stop us from fully experiencing life. We want a great life, just not now.

It's a victim mentality. People take offense to this label, but it's simply looking outside ourselves for answers. Surrendering our power to avoid responsibility. In the end, the root cause is fear. Waiting for the perfect time is a lie that steals dreams. The scary part is that the time may never come. Waiting leads to the pain of failure and regret, a high price to pay. Move forward a little each day. Clarity and confidence only come from forward movement.

Quote: "Things may come to those who wait, but only the things left by those who hustle." Abraham Lincoln, 16th President of the Unites States of America

Resource: *High-Performance Habits* by Brendon Burchard

Action Step: Are you waiting on anything? Journal on it. Then get out of your own way by taking the first step. Your confidence will increase, and you'll feel better.

I waited for over a year, which was out of character. I've always leaned towards action, even if it was a wasted effort. I was always in motion, even if I ran 100 mph in the wrong direction. I felt safe in movement. However, my confidence was shaken, and my business was suffering. I couldn't sell anything. I was failing.

I was trying to sell as opposed to serving others. I needed people to buy. I had commission breath.

I was devastated after every lost sale. The accusing voice, "You're losing it. You're not good anymore. This is the end," kept dominating my thoughts. I was losing the battle of my brain.

Since I couldn't sell, I shifted into management mode by telling others what to do. I was great at giving speeches but didn't lead by example. I needed to attend my own lectures. I was waiting for my team to make me successful. My ego convinced me that pushing others was the key to the next level. I stopped doing what initially created my success. It was an avoidance strategy. Instead of correcting my weaknesses, I got fixated on others. They had the same issue and couldn't close a sale. I was kicking the can down the road. My income was decreasing, and my shift in strategy was failing. It was time to face the music and upgrade my skills.

With my back against the wall, I went all in. I studied sales mentality and skills for several hours per week. I taught others. Most importantly, I faced my fear by getting back in the field. I became an example for my team. I started getting results, and my team began to believe they could succeed.

I never forgot the lesson to keep doing the things that created my success. Most importantly, I stopped waiting on others and ceased avoiding challenges. Instead, I resolved to face them immediately.

6. Don't Settle

As children, adults told us we could do anything. Dream big, go for it, don't give up. Usually, the adults instructing us stopped dreaming, never went for it, and gave up. So, we thought, why aren't they following their own advice? Which created doubt. If it were possible, wouldn't they be doing it? Yet, even without their example, we held on to our dreams. However, for most of us, our dreams eventually died.

Dreams are important but not urgent. Our lives are filled with urgency. It's the non-important things that steal our attention. Our smartphones are urgent, non-important weapons of mass distraction. What we cease thinking about eventually atrophies. Dreams are pushed into the future. Eventually, dream-killing thoughts creep in. "It's too late. I don't have the time. I've failed a lot in the past. What if I go all in and fail? It won't be worth it."

The dream dies as we stop believing in ourselves. We settle and compare ourselves to others. We live through our heroes in sports and on television. We live vicariously through our children. We hang out with others who settled. We talk about the weekend and our past glory days. We become addicted to comfort and count the days until retirement. We tell our kids to dream big, go for it, don't give up – and the cycle repeats.

Unfortunately, this strategy is unfulfilling. There is no happy ending to an unhappy journey. People who settle arrive safely at the end of their life, full of regrets. It's too big of a price to pay. Don't do it.

Quote: "The word settle is the most offensive word in the English language." – Monte Holm, Entrepreneur, Author, and Speaker

Resource: *The 177 Mental Toughness Secrets of the World Class* by Steve Siebold

Action Step: Journal:

1. What dream do you have?
2. What dream-killing thoughts have stopped you from pursuing it?
3. Write them down.
4. Refuse to allow these lies to kill your dream.
5. Take the next step forward.

I was frustrated with my corporate career. I worked constantly and traveled to many undesirable places. For years, my life was: wake up, go to work, come home, and go to bed. I was wandering aimlessly and lacking fulfillment. My purpose was busyness and trading time for money.

During my most challenging week, a turning point occurred. I had a difficult client with a looming deadline, and we were way behind. The deadline was the Monday after Easter and working on Easter Sunday was highly probable. Easter was my mom's favorite holiday. When I told her I would miss out, she gave me a look that only a mom could give. "You better be here. Figure it out!"

I figured it out. I worked 120 hours in 6 days without sleep and tons of coffee. We finished the job, and I arrived home at 11 p.m. on Saturday night. My brother and I lived together. He hadn't seen me in a week and wasn't sure what had happened. He asked THE question. "Is this really going to be your career? This is crazy." I was exhausted and didn't want to talk about it. However, the seed was planted.

The next day I spent several hours in silence with a journal, answering this question. What did I want my life to look like? I had never seriously thought about it. Then, I started dreaming for the first time. I wanted time, control, financial peace of mind, and freedom. I wanted to make an impact and have a purpose. I got excited about the possibilities but then became depressed. I looked at my career. I was an employee, and my time was theirs. I could do okay financially, but I would continue to depend on them. I would always be a few paychecks away from financial collapse. They controlled me.

I was helping our clients but not making an impact. I would only ever impact a few people in a meaningful way. As a result, I lacked purpose and was miserable. There would be nothing memorable about my life. The life I wanted couldn't happen as an employee, so I had to become an entrepreneur.

I reached the moment of truth and had a decision to make. I could either change and go after my dreams, or I could do what the masses do, give up, settle, and shrink the dream to match my reality. And then compare myself to others, trying to feel better because I was more successful than most people. It was completely unsatisfying. I would regret choosing comfort and settling, and it would haunt me until I died. I needed to give my dream life a legitimate shot.

I chose the uncomfortable path and became an entrepreneur. I took small steps and transformed my life and family forever. I am forever grateful that I had the courage to change.

7. You're Too Young to be Old

Our society views old age as a negative. Life expectancies continue to increase, yet the perception of aging diminishes. People negatively view their 50s – 80s. They believe their best is behind them, and they can no longer contribute. With time, these thoughts begin to manifest themselves. They retreat, unhappy and depressed. They stop growing and contributing. Their mental and physical health deteriorates, yet it doesn't have to be this way.

A study from the New England Journal of Medicine proves this point. Our most productive time is between 60-70 years of age. The second most productive time is between 70-80. The third is the 50-60 age group. The average age for presidents of prominent companies is 63. The average age for pastors of the largest 100 churches in the United States is 71. The average age for a Pope is 76.

The best years of our lives are between 50-80. You reach your prime at age 60 and it continues into your 80s. There are many reasons. At this stage of life, you know who you are and care less what others think. You have fewer distractions.

Shift your thinking and take heart. God's not done with you yet. Your best days are ahead. Stop retreating, get out, and contribute.

Quote: "You're never too old to become younger." – Mae West, Actress

Resource: *Too Young to Be Old, Love, Learn, Work and Play as you Age* by Nancy K Schlossberg, Ed.D.

TedX Talk – Lloyd Reeb – The Most Productive Years of your Life May Surprise You - www.youtube.com/watch?v=VfkBDRa9J1I

Action Step: Share this chapter with others. If you aren't in this age category, share it with someone who needs to hear it.

When I turned 50 years old, I had an epiphany. It was the first time I really connected to my mortality. I realized that I wasn't getting out of this thing alive. The thought was depressing. I fell into the "I'm old" thinking trap of the masses. However, I felt better at 50 than I had at 40 and I was at my best. I came across the New England Journal of Medicine study and immediately felt energized. I started sharing this with my clients and teammates. I could see an immediate shift in their energy. They were given an instant shot of hope.

I'm at a convention with 1,000 financial advisors a few weeks later. I'm asked to join a panel on stage. I get the intuitive insight to share this study. I asked everyone over 50 to shout out and heard two people murmur. It was shockingly quiet. Everyone was embarrassed or ashamed of being over the age of 50. So, I read the study, and it energized the crowd. At our reception, hundreds of people approached me, wanting a copy. It was as if they had a new lease on life. They were happy and excited. They no longer believed it was the end. They could contribute and grow. They were entering their prime with much left to do.

The next day, Sharon Lechter, co-author of Rich Dad Poor Dad, addressed the audience. She's a powerhouse and a world-class individual. She's in this age group and contributing more than ever. She presented this same study word-for-word. She wasn't there the night I talked about it. She had everyone stand up over the age of 50. This time, they were screaming loud and proud. The energy was different. I was blown away.

8. Don't Wrestle with Your Ego

Our ego keeps us stuck. It doesn't like growth and change. To succeed, we must master the ability to "think about what we think about" (metacognition). Awareness is essential. We feel it in our bodies when the ego is in control. Our hearts shut down, and we start spinning stories. A situation triggers us, and the ego takes over. It's not good.

Any action/reaction from this state can be destructive. The three most destructive thought patterns, the 3 Rs, take over: Resentment, Resistance, and Revenge. A negative thought toward another is a form of revenge. Ideas that move us to action can be devastating, especially if the other person is equally triggered. The key is to stop the momentum after the second R; resistance. Get a journal, and document the situation and what you're making up about it. We are storytellers. Getting this from our minds and onto paper is enlightening.

Create space around the situation for a few days, and then review what you wrote. You will swear someone else wrote it. Collecting this evidence proves that our ego is not rational. Knowing what triggers us is paramount to our success and peace of mind. It stops the potential disaster before it unravels. We avoid an egoic wrestling match, which saves us and others from unnecessary suffering. We can control our thinking and our emotions. This is a massive energy leak that deserves your attention.

Quote: "Never Wrestle with pigs (your ego) you both get dirty, and the pig likes it." – George Bernard Shaw, Irish Playwright

Resource: *Loving What Is* by Byron Katie. Google Byron's "Judge Your Neighbor" Worksheet. Use this as a resource to guide your journaling.

https://thework.com   or click here to go directly to their site:

Action Step: Journal:

1. Describe a situation that triggered your ego.
2. Use the "Judge Your Neighbor" worksheet as a guide.
3. Role-play to yourself a conversation with the other person.
4. Let yourself get petty.
5. Repeat until you become neutral about the situation.

I volunteered for a non-profit organization for two years and led one of its initiatives. They had a particular way of doing things. I had a high opinion of myself, and my ego was in control. I was doing things my way because I knew best, and they initially allowed it. However, I kept drifting further from their standard and started to hang myself. Finally, they requested a meeting to discuss the issue.

When the request was made, I got triggered. The root issue that triggers me is "I don't matter." If you don't take my advice, then "I don't matter" takes over. If you reject my recommendation, I don't matter. If I want to give to you, and you don't care, then that means I don't matter.

I discovered this mind virus from a coach, and my awareness increased. I improved at catching myself before losing control. But this time, it slipped by and took root. When I lose control, my chest tightens, my heart shuts down, and I start judging. The longer I'm in this state, the more psychological damage is done. The longer I'm in resistance, the harder it is to let go. I was in full-blown judgment. I knew writing a long attacking email would be problematic. I needed to let this go.

I started journaling about the situation. I allowed myself to get petty to ensure I got all my feelings out. I was offended. How dare they question me. Don't they know who I am? They only care about what they think. They don't appreciate me, screw them.

The emotion started to subside. Then I role-played the future meeting in my mind. I allowed myself to be angry and upset as I visualized the scene. I yelled at them and let them have it. I was self-righteous and told them what I thought of them. This brought the emotions up, and I fully released them.

In the past, I would've pushed the emotions down, and the volcano would've exploded. This created a lot of damage. This time, I couldn't do it as it would destroy two great friendships. The more times I role-played, the better I felt. Several days later, I re-read what I wrote. It's as if an alien had come into my body. I couldn't believe what I had journaled. I finally let it go. The meeting was a non-event. They explained why I needed to follow protocol. I had no emotion about it, and they were correct. I was creating a mess. I was serving only my ego and no one else.

I've done this exercise numerous times. I have tremendous evidence that my ego is insane. I've learned to not wrestle with the pig (ego), as that's what it wants me to do. I no longer take the bait and attempt to head off the egoic slide before it begins. It takes time, but it's worth it. This process has been invaluable to me.

I've avoided stupid business decisions and kept my mouth shut. It has saved relationships, created peace, and given me confidence. It's evidence that I can control my thinking and emotions.

9. Quitter's Relief is a Lie, Don't Fall for It

The masses can't quit the things they should and often quit the things they shouldn't.

We have an internal ceiling on what we believe is possible. We go after a goal and leave our comfort zone. We bump into the terror barrier, which is the threshold when we break past our old conditioning. Ego and fear take control, our fight or flight response is triggered, and a new level of discomfort occurs. Close to a breakthrough, we bounce off the barrier versus breaking through it. We go back to our old conditioning and feel relief from the bounce.

Like a rubber band being stretched, the tension is released. The relief is, "I'm glad that's over," or "I'm happy I don't have to do that anymore." IT'S A LIE. It's temporary, like a sugar high. It's sweet for a minute but is always followed by a crash.

Same with the quitter's relief lie. The initial relief is satisfying, but the crash follows. The crash in confidence and self-esteem. Even worse, your standards are reduced, and you settle.

Don't fall for it. Call your mentor. They've experienced it and broken through. Get their guidance. Remind yourself of why you're doing it. Don't hide like the masses. Get new insight and go after it again. Visualize how great it will feel on the other side. Repetition and persistence are key. Your future self will thank you for persisting.

Quote: "It's a slow process but quitting won't speed it up." –
Unknown

Resource: Bob Proctor YouTube Video: *Overcoming the Terror Barrier*

https://www.youtube.com/watch?v=P1LD9eGjQKM

Action Step:

1. Set an uncomfortable goal that will stretch you.
2. Identify why it's important.
3. Get a mentor and set a weekly accountability time.
4. Go after it.
5. You will know when you're up against the terror barrier.
6. Journal what you are making up about it and call your mentor when you feel like retreating.

I had bumped up against my self-imposed ceiling and was stuck for too long. Not only did I bounce against the terror barrier, but I was also retreating. Things were disintegrating on all fronts, and I had a pit in my stomach. I had many fears, but the main one was the fear of loss. Fear of losing my business, my marriage, and the little money I had.

There were many signs that I was retreating. I stopped paying attention to my results and became delusional. I played the victim by blaming outside circumstances for my issues. I looked to the future versus focusing on the task at hand. I stopped enjoying the process and began drifting. In my previous quitting experiences, it wasn't a sudden exit. It was a slow drift that wasn't noticeable.

I started thinking the grass was greener someplace else. A move elsewhere could relieve this unbearable tension and stress. I wasn't yet serious about quitting, but I was beginning to take those steps. I was looking for a problem-free business, which doesn't exist. I had to pivot, so I contacted a few mentors with an emergency email for help. I didn't like asking for help. I thought it made me look weak, which kept me broke and miserable.

They all got back to me quickly, and the calls changed my paradigm. Successful people are more than willing to help; they just never get asked. Those conversations changed my direction. They listened and let me whine.

They encouraged me and pointed out why I could do it. They reminded me that although quitting looked attractive, it would be devastating, and I would forever regret it. I would eventually face the same issue if I quit and went somewhere else. Just kicking the can down the road. They challenged and helped me take the next steps. It was uncomfortable, but quitting was more uncomfortable.

Giving up on my ideal life was non-negotiable. I almost got seduced by the quitter's relief lie. I'm forever grateful that I didn't.

10. Don't Retreat

Life can be challenging. We're disappointed by people who let us down, and we carry the baggage of past trauma. We take things personally and get emotional. We don't let go and can't forgive. We hold onto the drama and judge others for the same things we do.

Life would be easy if it wasn't for people. The ego isn't intelligent, but it is clever. If we can't let go, the ego stays in charge. Living in this chaotic state, we look to the future. We dream, "One day, I can chill and do nothing." The allure of retreating into our little bubble of comfort is appealing. In the bubble, we can't get hurt. There is no stress, and we can relax.

There are many escape mechanisms to choose from. We believe we will find joy in retreating. We convince ourselves to pull back and even quit. It's a trap; there's no joy in retreating. We stop growing and contributing and begin to decay mentally and physically. When we isolate ourselves, we're stuck with our own dysfunctional thoughts of delusion and judgment.

Since we never let go of the pain, we are trapped in the personal hell of past issues. Even in our bubble, the memories keep replaying. Wherever we go, we're always there. Old man ego is in control. It doesn't end well.

Stop retreating. Override the lie and get active. Find ways to contribute. Let go of the past, and forgive yourself and others. Go make an impact. Take the focus off you and serve others. When we focus on helping others, we experience joy. When we focus only on ourselves, it's a dead end. Don't retreat.

Quote: "If you have a setback, don't take a step back, get ready to make your comeback." Tim Story, Author & Speaker

Resource: Tappingsolution app.

Tapping is a powerful technology for permanently releasing negative emotions and baggage.   https://bit.ly/TappingAppLink

Action Step: Journal:
1. What am I focused on, and what must this be creating?
2. What retreating thoughts are you having?
3. Recognize the trap.
4. What can you do to give/contribute today?
5. Take the first step.

My back was against the wall, and the only option was to move forward. I had a vision to finally leave financial lack behind. I couldn't retreat or I would fail. It was difficult mentally and physically. I knew making a bold move would create a mess. I knew good and bad things would occur, but I had no other option.

We eventually hit our goals and helped a lot of people. It was an amazing feeling. The initial vision had come to pass, and it was time to celebrate. Party time was fun, but what was next? It was an unbelievable experience, yet with no new vision, I was stuck.

I was falling into the trap of retreating. I was intimate with retreating as I'd witnessed it many times. I had coached entrepreneurs through it and realized how easy it was to be deceived. "I don't want to work anymore. I don't want to keep showing up. I've worked hard, I deserve to chill." These are the dominant thoughts that lead to retreating. It's especially hard when you're no longer required to.

Rest and fun are necessary, but only temporarily. Fulfillment only comes from growth and service. It was time to reset a new vision for my life. I needed to avoid the mistakes of others. They would create a new vision and then stop.

Their bodies were rested but still mentally fatigued. Tired from carrying the past pain. They lacked the mental energy to execute the plan. The vision would be set aside, and they retreated. They stopped moving forward and became a shell of their former selves. They looked for fulfillment from the wrong sources. It was an endless, fruitless search.

I didn't want this. I needed to forgive and let go to create the necessary mental energy. I was holding onto past resentments and judgments. I worked on it every day and still do. I wrote down the names of people I needed to forgive. My name was on the list. It wasn't overnight, but I released the emotion. I let it go and cleaned the inside. I set a new vision to help millions of people free themselves mentally and financially, and I'm more excited than ever. I'm on high alert when the retreating signals start. It means I have work to do.

Do the work, don't ever retreat.

Pillar 2

The Shift

THINK&GROW
YOU

11. Take 100% Responsibility

It's easy to blame our lack of progress on outside circumstances. We make excuses, justifications, and validations about why we are stuck. We surrender our power to external forces. We avoid the internal work required to succeed and settle for comfort. We spend time hoping rather than doing the necessary work.

Taking 100% responsibility for our lives is the secret to significant, long-lasting success. It's the only way we can pivot and learn the lesson.

Quote: "When you think everything is someone else's fault, you will suffer a lot. When you realize that everything springs only from yourself, you will learn both peace and joy." – Dalai Lama.

Resource: *Untethered Soul: The Journey Beyond Yourself* by Michael Sinclair

Action Step: Think and journal:

1. In what area of your life have you not taken 100% responsibility?
2. Finances, health, relationships?
3. Pick 1 area and journal on what excuses you have been making.
4. Do you like the results?
5. What have you learned?
6. What is the first step to creating change?

In 2008, we struggled and went from owning a home to renting. Things continued getting worse and I still wasn't getting it. My cash flow was decreasing, and I ran out of places to borrow money.

At the end of July, I owed my ex-wife $5,200 in alimony and child support. I didn't have the money and was clueless about what to do.

I decided my only action plan was to try to convince my wife, Marlow, to use her savings to pay my ex-wife. It didn't go over well. Marlow lost it, threw her purse at me, and used every curse word in the book. "Volcanic Marlow" is not a pretty sight.

She couldn't figure out how I could be talented and broke. I asked her, "Why are we still married?" This was a mistake. She gave me the silent treatment and went upstairs to decide if she should stay or go.

This was the biggest turning point of my life. Wherever I've had a problem in my life, I've always been there. I was the common denominator of my failures. I created 100% of these problems. My business wouldn't survive, and I was staring down my second divorce.

It occurred to me that most of my family struggled financially, and it didn't matter that I was a CPA or financial advisor. The money beliefs I inherited from my family must be questioned and upgraded.

It's the first time I took 100% responsibility for my results. I had to change, and I had to be all in, just like an Olympic athlete. So that's what I did. The transformation wasn't overnight, but a few years later, our situation was unrecognizable.

12. Draw the Line in the Sand

Being addicted to comfort becomes familiar. We get comfortable with dysfunction and losing. We become like hypnotic robots and stop growing. We escape reality by retreating to our pleasure of choice.

Justifications, validations, and excuses dominate our thoughts. We justify being stuck and collect reasons for not moving forward. Meanwhile, no growth means we start disintegrating.

We reject reality so we don't feel bad. The less we look, the worse it gets. It takes a jolt to wake us up and we have a reality check. We finally connect the dots with who's paying the price for our delusion. We suffer as well as our loved ones and the price is too high.

We shift and start thinking critically. We pull on latent resources. We get creative and move from desperation to determination. We evolve. We draw a line in the sand representing a point of no return.

It's a place in history not worth revisiting. When the decision is made, the past stops repeating. The chapter is closed. A new day is here.

Quote: "Sometimes you just have to draw a line in the sand and say enough is enough." – Unknown

Resource: *Quantum Success* by Sandra Anne Taylor

Action Step: Journal:

1. What dysfunctional situation have you tolerated for way too long?
2. Draw a line in the sand.
3. What's the first step to moving forward?

The day after our biggest fight, Marlow and I decided to stay married and avoid bankruptcy. For the first time, we set a big goal together.

A game plan was created with a weekly progress check-in. She was going to interview wealthy couples and learn their secrets. I was going to relentlessly work on changing my money beliefs.

We assessed the current situation. Marlow laid out the bloody balance sheet, income statement, and budget. For the first time, I looked at the big picture from a place of acceptance. I didn't need to love it, but I had to stop hating it.

Change can only happen from acceptance. No more "This shouldn't be happening." I forgave myself. No more guilt or shame. I looked at Marlow and said, "We will never be back here again!"

The line in the sand moment. Decision made. I was all in. Why didn't I do this before? It was a powerful declaration. I knew things would be different. We made a total commitment, and it was the beginning of a miraculous financial transformation.

13. You Deserve It

People suffer from the "I don't deserve" mind virus. Telling themselves, "I don't deserve happiness, love, success, or money." It's an endless list.

It's a man-made mind virus. Nature doesn't have a deserving issue. Animals believe they deserve to thrive, and trees believe they should grow. Only man can create something that opposes nature.

However, most of us buy the lie. The sad part is we can go our entire lives and never question it. We show up as perfect little babies with no deserving issues. We deserve to be loved, cared for, and protected. We cried when we wanted something and didn't hesitate out of fear. We were in harmony with nature, and our needs were met.

Then at some point, we made a mistake. We were told we were bad, not good enough, or less than others. These lies created a belief. Anchored with this false judgment, we attracted situations to prove it.

The symptom manifests itself as a lack of money, love, and happiness. The root of all deserving issues is a lack of self-forgiveness, and we must start there. We must forgive ourselves for past mistakes.

Perfection is another lie. We are a miracle and a mess at the same time. The sooner we accept that, the better our lives can be. We deserve an amazing life. It's time to release the virus and affirm the best.

Quote: "We are a miracle and a mess at the same time." – Jonathan Manske, Author, Speaker.

Resource: *The Think & Grow Rich Action Pack* by Napoleon Hill

Action Step: Journal:

1. What worthiness stories do you have?

2. Write it out. It's a lie. This pattern will continue until you quit paying attention to it.

3. Write out the opposite of that lie in as much detail as you can.

4. When the lie comes up, shift and focus your thoughts on what you want.

I grew up constantly comparing myself to others. Some of my friends appeared to have it all. The perfect home life with money and opportunities. More smarts and greater athletic ability.

This experience continued into college. I was broke and envied those with wealth and advantages. Subconsciously, I viewed myself as average and created the story that others, not me, deserved great success. My belief created my reality. I believed that I didn't deserve a great life. I would be okay but mostly struggle.

At a conscious level, I had a burning desire to excel, and I matched that with a great work ethic. It helped me with my first job. I had something to prove. I experienced corporate career success and then started my own entrepreneurial venture.

There were challenges and successes. I was focused and hardworking, yet always broke. I was constantly outrunning the bill collector and acquiring more debt.

In my personal development journey, I finally discovered the mental block. I didn't deserve to be wealthy. I studied worthiness issues and discovered they were lies.

I didn't need to hire a therapist to pull the scab off. I needed to stop giving it power. When it would come up, I didn't fight it because that's what the lie wanted me to do. I would simply smile. "There's that old story again." I would redirect my thoughts to an affirmation or scripture. I stopped searching for proof of the lie. What you ignore atrophies. I'm not sure when it happened, but the limiting belief eventually disappeared. It no longer controlled me.

14. Get Emotional

We're taught logical goal-setting skills that usually miss the mark. The secret to inspiration is uncovering our emotional motivators, as we are driven by our desire to feel a certain way. Once those feelings are identified, energy moves towards their fulfillment. The stronger the feeling, the greater our persistence.

Obstacles are no match for an emotionally fueled mind. This biologically based strategy is the foundation of success. It's the antidote for rejection, frustration, and disapproval. When harnessed correctly, emotional energy is unstoppable. Just imagining the desired feeling creates a level of power that logic is incapable of.

Quote: "Don't make excuses for why you can't get it done. Focus on all the reasons why you must make it happen." – Ralph Marston, Author

Resource: *The Ultimate Secrets of Total Self-Confidence* by Dr. Robert Anthony

Action Step: Journal:
1. What is your #1 goal?
2. What are your biggest emotional reasons for achieving it?
3. What is the #1 feeling you're hoping to attain?

As a CPA, my logical brain dominated. I thought I was a great goal-setter. My plans were on spreadsheets with lots of numbers and data. I loved mapping everything out, but the problem was, I worked hard and still failed. Excessive planning was masking my fear of taking action.

During our worst financial hardship, Marlow and I set a big savings goal. I wanted to analyze everything but realized this familiar path would fail. So instead of analyzing first, we invested the time discussing why the goal was important and how we wanted to feel.

There were many emotion-based reasons. We never wanted to fight about money. I wanted to feel peace. I wanted see my kids more and feel like a good father. We wanted to be an example and teach others.

To feel this way, we had to be financially stable, and that's what we did. The desire to experience these specific feelings fueled our efforts. That's the power of getting emotional.

15. Get Aligned

When our conscious and unconscious minds disagree, we fight ourselves. For example, we want to be wealthy at a conscious level, but unconsciously believing money is bad keeps us broke. Changes must occur at the deeper unconscious level.

When these two levels agree, we succeed. We know we are good (conscious), and it's confirmed in our hearts (unconscious). It's a knowing that is irrefutable. This is an internal mastermind.

We also align with a higher power. Depending on your beliefs, it's called: God, Source, or Infinite Intelligence. When aligned, things work easier, and we're in a flow state. There is no stress or struggle, and we reach a powerful state called enthusiasm.

Enthusiasm is joy combined with a goal. Consciously, you're going after the goal, and unconsciously, you believe it will happen. As a result, your thinking is elevated to another level. Spirit is speaking to you in a soft voice, and the loud voice of your ego is muted. You're being guided by intuition and trusting it.

Your energy is elevated, and you look like a maniac to the onlooker. Internally, you're in utopia. You're alive and unleashed, and nothing is holding you back. You're an arrow flying effortlessly to your target and adding massive value to others. You're in a powerful place of helping others and getting rewarded. It's an amazing feeling.

The secondary reward is the goal. The primary is being fully alive. Your self-development plan is the key that unlocks this energy.

Releasing beliefs that no longer serve you is paramount. You're freed up when you stop running a marathon with a 20lb bowling ball tied to your ankle. It's work to remove the garbage, but it's worth it. Unfortunately, most never do the work to align themselves as they wait for the outside world to change. They might get rewarded, but it's short-lived. They never experience the reward of enthusiasm. Do the work and get aligned. It's worth every second.

Quote: "Your mind is the most fertile acreage in the world. Millions of acres. How do you think your life will turn out if you are only weeding it a few minutes per day?" – Coach Roy Dayton, Success Coach.

Resource: Convergence Seminars
www.convergenceseminars.com

Action Step: Journal:
1. When was a time you were enthusiastic and you nailed a goal?
2. How were you feeling?
3. How did you show up?
4. Write this down and begin being this way and watch what happens.

I'm grateful to be involved in an entrepreneurial venture where all promotions are results based, not subjective. However, there is frustration when you don't advance. I was stuck at the same level for eight years. I was waiting for something to change externally; the economy, my team, our company. I was stubborn and this approach didn't work.

After hitting the brick wall again, I finally realized I had to change. I had to go all in on my personal growth. I tackled a long list of limiting beliefs, one at a time. I gave myself grace. My head and heart needed to become aligned if I was going to succeed.

I worked on forgiveness and worthiness issues. I began to value myself and appreciate others. I sold myself on the value I delivered. I worked on my money head trash. I leveled up spiritually. I watched my internal dialogue and paid attention to what I verbally communicated.

I spotted limiting beliefs based on my verbiage and worked to release those lies. I eliminate the words' try,' 'but,' and 'can't' from my vocabulary. I stopped making excuses for my lack of progress.

It wasn't overnight, but I was becoming internally aligned. We set a goal to reach the next promotion level, which I previously never thought was possible. I still didn't fully believe it, but I was in a better place. The target date was June 30th, and I was all in.

It was a huge move for our team, and we were behind. Then, on May 27th, I was working out when a small voice hit me like a lightning bolt. "It can happen this month." A full month sooner? We were way behind, but I was getting much better at trusting this voice. I also knew I needed to act before my ego killed the idea.

I stopped the workout, ran upstairs, and told Marlow. We didn't know how but trusted the intuitive guidance.

I showered and went to the office. I cleared the decks and called clients and teammates. I was fully aligned and enthusiastic. In my heart, I knew we would hit it. I looked like a madman on a mission.

What happened over the next several days was jaw-dropping. We hit the goal that had eluded us for eight years and surpassed it by only $456 in revenue! We helped a bunch of people in the process. It felt great to hit the goal, and my belief soared. The real reward was the experience. It was confirmation that all the work was worth it. I never doubted it again.

16. What If Up?

We're taught to hope for the best but prepare for the worst. "Don't get your hopes up so you won't be disappointed." We don't get what we hope for but what we expect.

Our minds tend to spin negative stories. "What if my business fails? What if I lose my job? What if the economy goes south? What if something happens to my family?" We are trapped by the wasted emotion of worry.

We stay stuck. We waste time and energy obsessing over worst-case scenarios. We believe if we're prepared for the worst, we won't be surprised when bad things happen. It creates a cycle of unhappiness. What we focus on grows. We begin searching and attracting situations to support our pessimistic view.

"What if down?" doesn't work. What if we expected the best? How would our lives change? It takes work to shift to "What if up?" What do you have to lose? Give "What if up?" a shot.

Quote: "What if your life is falling together vs. falling apart?" – Jonathan Manske, Author, Speaker, Cerebral Sanitation Engineer

Resource: *The Law of Attraction Made Simple* by Jonathan Manske

Action Step: Journal:

1. What is your #1 goal?
2. Frequently use the "What if" concept as a daily affirmation. The tool is especially useful when doubts creep in. Interrupt the pattern with "what if?"

I was desperate and looking for answers. I scraped together money to hire a mindset guru. I wanted guidance on doubling our income, which would get us back to financial break even.

During our coaching session, He asked a ton of questions, then would sit in silence like Yoda. It was a strange experience for a recovering CPA. I was looking for techniques and strategies. The fact that my thoughts created my reality still wasn't registering. After 90 minutes, I expected some amazing insight.

All he said was, "So, if you want to double your income, just say 'What if I make $X amount?' multiple times per day. Your mind can't dismiss a 'what if' statement. It will eventually click, and you will believe you can do it."

I was stunned and couldn't believe I had just wasted $375. He then said, "It's so simple you probably won't do it."

He challenged me with those words, and I had nothing to lose. I started using "what if" hundreds of times a day. "What if my cash flow was $X, what if our net worth was $X? What if I was financially independent? What if I was happy? What if I was successful?"

Eventually, "what if" shifted to "I am the person that does this." The internal shift happened, and it was only a matter of time before the outside results matched.

This became my go-to affirmation for almost everything. When I didn't feel good, what if I did? I eventually what if'd my way to more success and fulfillment.

We hit those impossible goals and surpassed them, and I learned a valuable lesson. When you set a goal, it isn't necessary initially to believe it's possible. You can grow your belief over time. The "what if" tool transformed my beliefs and results.

17. Grow Spiritually

Tapping into our spiritual side is a must. Spirituality strengthens our outlook for a better future. We are spirit, yet many deny it. As a result, many people live in their intellect and disregard their spirit. Growing spiritually is paramount to achieving our ideal life.

The conditions of trust, joy, love, acceptance, and forgiveness all happen from our spiritual side. Spiritual growth enhances our ability to deal with the challenges of life. It allows us to relate to others with compassion and understanding.

Our spirit focuses on serving others. It makes us feel that life is worthwhile, and we aren't some random mistake. We are here for a reason and meant to contribute.

When we grow spiritually, we learn to see the beauty and wonder of life. The denial of our spiritual side robs us of peace and fulfillment. The search to fill this hole by other means is never-ending. We will always feel like something is missing.

Quote: "Most importantly, the meaning of spirituality lays the seeds for our destiny and the path we must follow" – Dennis Banks, Native American Activist, Author

Resource: *Around the Year* by Emmet Fox

Action Step:

1. Reach out to someone you admire who is living the life you want.
2. Schedule a time to interview him or her on spirituality.
3. Apply what resonates with you.

I've always believed there was something greater than the physical realm. Yet, my experience with religion as a child was unsettling. A few times, I was dragged to churches where the sermons were dominated by sin, fear, and guilt. I felt worse leaving than when I showed up, and it turned me off to organized religion.

However, I often prayed before sporting events. I prayed before bed and prior to meetings and speaking engagements. I prayed for a peaceful resolution to the chaos in my life. I started reading New Age authors and studied law of attraction concepts. It made sense to me.

I would get criticized by the judgmental religious crowd for reading the wrong things. They were trying to fix me. It seemed they had much to fix in their lives, but it was easier to focus on me. Their self-righteousness pushed me further away. They weren't living the results I wanted, so I shook it off.

I was on my path, and things were unfolding. I studied Jesus and his ministry. I read, prayed, meditated daily, and slowly cleared years of baggage. I released guilt, shame, and lack of forgiveness for myself and others. I transformed.

This was a map that led me to become a Christian. I started reading a plain English Bible that a friend gave me. I read two pages a day. One day on a run, I received intuitive guidance to "Get Baptized!" I took immediate action and called our Pastor, who had married Marlow and me. I told him I wanted something simple, and we set the date. He baptized me at the pool in his condo complex. Just me and him. It was a life-altering experience, and I was never the same.

Both Christians and non-Christians ask me how I apply spirituality to my life. I'm happy to guide and help them on their journey. I don't judge their path or beliefs. To me, it's all about love, forgiveness, service, and peace. It's about a relationship, not a religion. Of all the growth I experienced, my spirituality has been the most pronounced and the foundation of my peace. Your religion of choice doesn't matter. It's your path. Stay on it, trust yourself and connect to it every day. You'll be thankful you did.

18. Trust Your Gut

Many of us suffer from indecision. We don't trust ourselves to choose wisely. The truth is most of us were never taught how to make decisions, and the root cause of indecision is fear.

The default projection of the average mind is failure, or what could go wrong versus right. We eagerly accept this line of thought as a protection mechanism. It helps us keep our emotions in check and our failures to a minimum. This risk-averse approach is both comforting and limiting and must be transcended if one is to ever attain an uncommon level of success.

Decisiveness is a mental muscle. It must be developed. The more decisions you make, the more decisive you become. Forgive yourself for the failures and applaud yourself for the successes. And while no one makes the correct decision every time, the best decision-makers among us are courageous enough to try.

Only you know what's best for you, not others and not society. Making decisions, especially bold decisions, means making mistakes. And the sooner you learn to live with the mistakes, the sooner you will enjoy the successes.

Quote: "Be decisive. A wrong decision is generally less disastrous than indecision." – Bernhard Langer, Professional Golfer.

Resource: *The Five Second Rule* by Mel Robbins

Action Step: Before making your next complex decision, employ the Ben Franklin Pros/Cons Method. Draw a T-chart; list the positives on the left and the negatives on the right. Whatever side outweighs the other is the winner. Trust it, decide, and take a small action to move forward. Don't question it; you can always course correct.

My wife and I were living in a small home in Central Denver. We were stressed financially and starving for answers. I managed the household finances, which were a complete disaster. $250,000 of credit card debt and thousands in negative monthly cash flow. We were at the end of our financial rope.

My wife, Marlow, did not know the situation, and I wanted it that way. She wanted to take control of the finances, but my self-righteous ego kept pushing her away. I decided to fix it, and the best way to gain clarity was through meditation. I wanted to clear my mind and ask for guidance, and the garage was the only place to meditate. So, in the middle of winter in Denver, I put on my ski parka, sat in my car, and calmed my mind. While meditating, the message from God was loud and clear: Let Marlow handle the money.

The message was received, and I knew I must act quickly. I moved immediately before my ego talked me out of it. I told Marlow the "Home CFO" position was now hers. She was stunned. She never believed I would give up control. Some pain ensued, but it was the best financial decision I ever made.

19. Acknowledge Yourself

Most of us weren't taught to acknowledge our accomplishments. Only our flaws and mistakes were highlighted. We must fix our weaknesses. We were told, "Don't get too full of yourself. Bragging is an ugly look."

We compare ourselves to others with more success. Compared to them, we haven't done squat. Our accomplishments aren't good enough. We beat ourselves up.

We believe that basking in the glow of our greatness is a flaw and conceited. We'll become lazy and weak. We'll lose our hunger. Our minds naturally focus on what we haven't done and our mistakes. It's easier to beat ourselves up than to give ourselves credit.

We tell ourselves that one day we will be happy. Once we climb that mountain, we can give ourselves some love and take it all in. Then we can stop and smell the roses. It never happens. We live our lives on the layaway plan and delay happiness.

We hit the mountain top, breathe, and then look to the next mountain. We might achieve, but the journey is no fun. There is no happy ending to an unhappy journey. We get older and regret the lost moments. We missed life while looking for a better life.

It's no way to live. We're all climbing a mountain, and it's okay to stop, look back and see how far we've come. We should acknowledge what we've done. Soak it in. Love and acknowledge ourselves. Take a mental snapshot and record the memory. It's the energy we need to continue. What are we waiting for?

Quote: "Quit staring at the pothole in Maui. It's ugly, and you end up missing all of Maui." – Coach Roy Dayton, Success Coach.

Resource: *I Am Enough* YouTube video(s) by Marissa Peer

Action Step:

1. Download the Winstreak app.
2. Set the goal to record three or more wins per day, large or small.
3. Review at the end of the day. Take it in, and acknowledge yourself.
4. At the end of the year, review what you wrote daily and record the most meaningful events in a journal. You'll be amazed at what you accomplished.

Being goal-focused, I'm always striving. Chasing the next mountaintop. It can be a struggle for me to appreciate where my feet are. I can get trapped in the "I'm not there yet" mindset, always running and missing blessings.

Marlow and I were in a week-long conference at a beautiful ranch. We were prospering, and the blessings were flowing. The transformation was mind-blowing. In a few short years, our lives were unrecognizable.

During the lunch break, I went on a walk. Taking in the beautiful scenery, I finally took time to reflect. I thought about what we left behind. The fear, scarcity, and stress. All the obstacles we overcame and the messes we cleaned up. The baggage we released and the growth we experienced. It was amazing to think about. Most would've quit countless times, but we didn't. We stayed strong and persevered.

With years of guilt gone, I was no longer beating myself up. Finally, a quiet voice spoke, "Good job Chris Felton." I felt it deeply and broke down crying. I'd never given myself credit. I feared I would become egotistical or I would lose my edge. Perhaps I hadn't done anything big enough to deserve it.

Many others gave me recognition and love, but I never did until now. Filled with goosebumps, it was one of the greatest feelings of my life. I started the habit of acknowledging the good in my life daily. It's the fuel that keeps me energized.

20. Trust, It's Going to Be Okay

Many of us were programmed to expect the worst. "The good times can't last forever. When is the other shoe going to drop? Save for a rainy day, get an emergency fund." We then find emergencies to deplete it.

"Batten down the hatches, brace yourself; the storm is coming." Worry prepares us for bad things. "Don't expect too much because you will be disappointed." Fear, doubt, and worry sell well in the media, while positive and uplifting isn't popular.

We search for evidence to support our view. What we focus on, we find. The masses hope for positive but expect negative. We get what we expect, not what we hope for.

Life can be difficult, and things happen, but they don't happen forever. It feels like it won't end, but it always does. Our biggest fear is that whatever happens, we won't be able to handle it. We can handle it.

We must do the mental work to expect a better life. We must become aware of our worry patterns and intervene. Otherwise, it becomes a self-fulfilling prophecy as we attract the results we feared.

Trust is the anchor, and it delivers. When we've succeeded, we've trusted. We must engage in thoughts of trust to get the desired result. It's not a setback but a setup.

Whatever is happening is necessary for us to grow. The resistance creates new muscles. Our response to the event will determine the result. Trust that your life is falling together, not falling apart. It's going to be okay.

Quote: "When your major goal is to live with optimism and trust, your other desires will be met." – Sandra Anne Taylor, Author

Resource: *Power Prosperity Podcast* by Randy Gage

Action Step:
1. Develop your trust muscles.
2. Journal your thoughts. What are your worry patterns? Recognizing these will help you stop and intervene when doom and gloom thinking arises.
3. Plant new seeds with scripture or affirmations.

My life was turning around, and our business was moving in the right direction. We saved money for the first time and bought our first home together. It was my favorite home. Not because it was the most luxurious or beautiful but because of what it meant.

Marlow and I stopped trying to fix each other and locked arms. We set a unifying goal and sacrificed to save for the down payment. We eliminated frivolous spending and watched every dollar. We had savings after the home purchase. It was a major turning point in our lives.

I'm grateful that Marlow recognized the importance of me visiting my kids. We allocated funds so I could see them every 5-6 weeks. It was one of the greatest investments in my life.

I was in town for my boys' baseball tournament. Caden and Carson were nine and six. They both were in the championship game for their respective teams. My ex had remarried and was deservingly happy.

Before the championship game, she asked that I stop by with them. They were dressed out. Caden in his red, white, and blue Twins uniform; Carson in his purple and gold Astros uniform. We arrived, and I was invited to sit in the kitchen for the first time.

She did a ritual with the boys before every game. She blared Katie Perry's "Firework" song, and the three of them danced together. The boys took turns holding mom's hands and dancing while singing those uplifting lyrics. They loved every moment of it. The looks on their faces as they looked up at mom, with the gigantic smiles, said it all. They were loved, and they knew it.

It had all turned around. The chapter of pain and struggle was closed. They were going to be okay; I was going to be okay.

It was a magical moment forever etched in my memory. At that moment, I realized how much time and energy I had wasted worrying. Things started changing when I trusted that it would be okay. Trust was the key that unlocked the blessings.

It's been many years since, but every time I hear that song, I am reduced to a puddle of tears. That song represented the beginning of a new chapter, and I am forever grateful.

21. Stop Resisting

Everyone has financial, career, health, family, and relationship stressors. What we resist will persist. Resistance is "this should not be happening." It's our mental battle with reality. Fear expresses itself as anger, frustration, guilt, procrastination, delusion, apathy, and blame.

We believe the more we obsess over an issue, the more likely we will solve it. Sometimes problems can grow and remain in our lives for years. As a result, we feel frustrated and helpless.

For example, we get a flat tire, and our first reaction is, "Why does this always happen to me? This shouldn't be happening! Who didn't fix that pothole?"

These statements resist the reality of a flat tire. We waste time denying reality before finally accepting, "We have a flat tire."

The flat tire doesn't care. The quicker we face reality and accept the situation, the quicker we fix the tire and move forward. Shifting from resistance to acceptance allows us to reframe the event. Acceptance fosters creativity. We choose a different action that leads to a better result.

Quote: "When you have a problem with the problem, now you have two problems." – Michael Sinclair, Author, Speaker

Resource: Attend Psi Seminars www.psiseminars.com

Read *The Sedona Method* by Hale Dwoskin

Action Step: Journal:

1. What's one area in your life that you wish was different?
2. What are your feelings?
3. How long has the problem existed?
4. Use the Sedona Method
   a. Identify your emotions and feel them.
   b. Ask/Answer 1. "Could I let it go?" Yes or No
   c. Would I let it go? Yes or No
   d. When? Now or later?
   e. Repeat the process until you feel a release of emotion.

When my kids were young, my ex-wife married a great guy, and the kids loved him. I felt guilty and replaced. Someone else was raising my kids. I told myself not to worry as they would know their real dad. I had a hard time convincing myself and suffered emotionally.

I finally started letting go of things I couldn't control. Releasing the "this shouldn't be this way" thinking and moving into acceptance. I discovered tools to help me process these negative feelings.

And it started to work until I was tested.

During a Christmas trip to see my kids, my 5-year-old (Carson) told me he was sad and missed his stepdad. My heart sank. All those negative emotions came rushing in. I knew I had to overcome this, or the trip would be ruined.

So, I focused on what Carson said, felt the feelings, and then asked myself three questions: Could I let it go? Would I let it go? When would I let it go?

I repeated this process for 10 minutes, and the feeling shifted from negative to neutral. My perspective changed. He was their stepdad; I couldn't control that. He was a great guy, and this was a benefit. It was about them and their well-being. I was making it all about me and decided to let it go.

The trip was amazing. When the kids mentioned their stepdad, no emotion came up.

All I've ever felt for their stepdad is appreciation. He's a fantastic role model and has helped them tremendously. He's an infinitely better husband to their mom than I ever was. When my kids leave their house, they tell him they love him, and he says it back. It's beautiful. I've never had a negative thought about him. I am forever grateful for him, and as a result, my boys have prospered. My relationship with them has continued to be strong and close.

22. Don't Label Things as Good or Bad

The masses allow the outside world to dictate their lives. Their environment creates their thoughts, feelings, and actions. If something good happens, they're happy; if something bad happens, they're depressed. They're a beach ball on the ocean of life.

This is the victim approach, yet people take offense to this word. Victim means blaming the outside world for how we feel and our results. Surrendering our power to outside forces. We don't want to change. We want the world to change.

Inordinate time is spent manipulating the circumstances in our lives. It's a massive energy leak, and it's exhausting. We immediately judge things as good or bad and our response to any event determines the outcome. "Why does this always happen to me?" and "Why can't I get a break?" are the disempowering questions of the victim.

Suspend judgment of whether it's good or bad, and don't label it. Be open to the blessing behind it, albeit you might not know for a while. Redirect your thoughts from doomsday thinking and stay emotionally neutral. Spend time thinking and listening to your intuition for the next step to make it positive.

Quote: "You cannot see the way out of a challenge if you are looking at it from the same level of mind, emotions, thoughts, and feelings of the past." – Dr. Joe Dispenza, Author.

Resource: *Breaking the Habit of Being Yourself* by Dr. Joe Dispenza

Action Step:
1. Think of past adversity you overcame.
2. Journal your initial reaction and thoughts.
3. What were the blessings that came out of it?
4. Resolve to change your response to challenges and stop labeling things as bad. Suspend your judgment.

I played the victim for most of my life, consumed by disempowering thoughts that battled reality. I used willpower to overcome these mental barriers, and it was a grind.

In my entrepreneurial venture, I initially operated from fear and worry. Some good things happened, but the happiness was short-lived. Many challenges and "bad things" occurred. I judged every situation from the lens of my past.

I was always putting out fires, and negative events would impact me emotionally for weeks. I was exhausted. I worked constantly, but it was mainly the mental energy drain that created the exhaustion. I got what I focused on. I fixated on problems and got them in spades. This had to change.

During our personal financial crisis, one of our top agents quit. He moved out of our office over the weekend. That Saturday, Marlow went to the office. I was coming in but stopped to hit some golf balls. She called me and told me what had happened. This was a financial blow to us. We had no financial wiggle room, and we lost a great guy.

Marlow said, "This is bad, what are we going to do?" My response had to be different. I said, "I don't know if this is bad, I'm going to suspend my judgment. It might actually be good." She said,

"Don't give me your law of attraction mumbo jumbo, this is bad. We lost a great producer and a renter. Our office lease is sucking us dry. This blows."

I gave her a similar "it might be good" response, and she hung up on me. I continued hitting golf balls, asking myself, where is the good? I stayed calm, and the answer came. He had a team of people, and I would reach out and let them know it was their lucky day as they now got to work with me. I did 20+ calls, emails, and multiple follow-ups with no response from anyone. They didn't care. Finally, I got a response from a 19-year-old kid who was excited and ready to go.

We scheduled a meeting to strategize. He showed up at my office wearing a clip-on tie with a big metal briefcase. I asked internally, "God, what do you want me to do here?" I didn't judge the situation, and we got after it. This relationship has been a miracle. He's become one of our best and most talented agents. His whole family came on board. He and his team have blessed thousands of people. It forever shifted the financial foundation of his family.

Years later, I was on appointments with his dad. He was dropping me off. As I was getting out, he grabbed my hand and said, "Chris, I am forever grateful that you showed up in our lives. You have no idea how much you have impacted my family. I don't know how I can repay you. Thank you so much. I love you brother."

We both had tears in our eyes; I'll never forget it. This wouldn't have happened if that original agent had stayed. This family would've been left behind. I'm grateful I suspended judgment and focused on the next step. The ripple effect continues.

Pillar 3

Relationships

23. Don't Be an Approval Addict

The need to please others is an obstacle to success. The stronger our need, the less success we will experience. In childhood, adults of influence reward us for doing what we're told. In exchange for compliance, they shower us with what we want. Gaining approval works for us as children, so we carry it into adulthood. If we follow a conventional path, it works our entire lives.

The trouble begins when we attempt to take a non-traditional route to success, such as becoming an artist, entrepreneur, or professional athlete. These paths are paved with failure, so to protect us, the important people in our lives often handicap us with disapproval. Due to years of seeking acceptance, many of us develop an unhealthy condition known as approval addiction. Like alcohol and drugs, approval addiction is an insidious condition that lies latent until triggered by disapproval. The impact on relationships, finances, and health can be severe.

Approval addiction can appear in many ways, such as not asking for what we want. We fear having difficult conversations, telling the truth, or asking for a sale. We spend money to impress others. These are only a few of the adverse side effects of this psychological disease.

The cure for approval addiction in medical circles is known as "systematic desensitization." This is the consistent exposure to the disapproval event that eventually leads to emotional desensitization. This frees us to properly pursue our passions. While we may continue to prefer approval, we no longer need it. This escape from the bondage of acceptance helps us transcend the fear of taking risks. It clears our path to greater success and fulfillment.

Quote: "Your need for the approval of others is the biggest check you'll ever write." – David Sandler, Founder, Sandler Training

Resource: *Defeating Approval Addiction Through Mental Toughness Training*, www.mtuec.com video training course led by Steve Siebold

Action Step: Journal:
1. How does approval addiction show up in your life?
2. Who pays the price for this?
3. Resolve to interrupt the approval pattern and continue doing what you fear until it's no longer an issue.

Since childhood, I sought approval from everyone. I was a full-blown approval addict. However, I didn't know I had a problem. Looking for answers to my stressful life, I decided to attend a seminar. In the process, I realized that I never got my dad's approval. At this point in my life, I didn't think I needed it, but upon further examination, I realized I was mistaken.

During one of the exercises, the facilitator said to me, "it's exhausting watching you attempting to gain the approval of the other seminar participants." He asked me, "Who in your life pays the price for your need for approval?"

It was a question that changed my life. The ones paying the price were: my kids, spouse, ex-wife, my team, clients—everyone. I sought the approval of everyone around me, and it was costing me (and them) dearly.

The facilitator continued pushing and said: "Your payoff is that you get to feed the addiction, but at what expense? Is the addiction worth it?"

I didn't like what he said, but I knew he was right. I knew what I had to do, and I knew I would do it. It was time for me to grow up and stop worrying about what everyone else thought about me.

So that's what I did, and slowly but surely, my life began to change. My entire world transformed before my eyes as I started seeing myself and my life differently. I let go of wondering how I appeared to others and focused on how I appeared to myself. I got tougher on myself and easier on others.

Over the next few years, my relationship with my kids improved. My marriage improved, and together, we built a thriving business. Today, I'm more excited about my life than ever, and it all started with breaking this formidable, yet silly, addiction.

24. Forgive

Forgiveness frees us from psychological bonds, yet it shouldn't be mistaken for condonation. Forgiveness means releasing the emotional energy employed in harnessing resentment. It has little to do with the perpetrator. It's not our job to be the karma police. Instead, forgiveness allows us to reclaim our power and reinterpret the activating event.

Lack of forgiveness diminishes us. We may experience it as unworthiness, poor decision-making, or self-doubt.

When we see someone as guilty, we're often projecting our own guilt. What we focus on grows. It's difficult to forgive ourselves unless we're willing to forgive others. Only through forgiveness can we release guilt.

Choose to let go of all of the negative perceptions of yourself and others. To be free, we must forgive. The ultimate goal is internal peace, and forgiveness is the way.

Quote: "To Forgive is to let a prisoner free and discover the prisoner was you." – Lewis B Smedes, Author

Resource: *Teach Only Love* by Dr. Gerald Jampolsky

Action Step:

1. Make a list of everyone against whom you hold a grievance.
2. List your thoughts concerning each grievance. This will provide a look into your own ego. The thoughts you have about yourself you will often see in others.
3. Begin the process of forgiving them and yourself.

I was at the end of my financial rope. Begrudgingly, I hired a coach. I thought I was mentally tough and only needed strategy & tactics to improve our financial situation, but I was wrong.

Early on, the coach threw me a curveball by asking me to forgive my ex-wife. I thought it was impossible. He informed me that my non-compliance was unacceptable. He instructed me to write down everything I admired about her.

For over an hour, I struggled, staring at a blank piece of paper. The resentment had a significant grip on me, but I stuck with the process. Eventually, it occurred to me that she was a good mom. No, I thought, a world-class mom. Our kids are amazing. They are thriving, and without her, there's no way this would've happened. In fact, I believe the kids needed to get away from dad while I cleaned up my act. I started focusing on this, and I felt better.

I repeated this exercise every day until I no longer needed it. Within months, my whole view of her changed. We chatted during the kid's baseball games, caught up on each other's lives, and discussed the kids.

What was once a grueling experience elevated into a pleasant conversation. The stressful alimony payments and child support, exacerbated by resentment, transformed into a positive investment. This money allowed her to stay at home and raise the kids. It was my best investment.

Marlow, my second wife, agreed that we would cease making negative comments about my first wife and never wavered from that commitment. The blessings that have flowed from this could fill another book, and it all started with a simple exercise that broke this destructive pattern.

25. Stop Controlling

We want to control circumstances out of fear and anxiety. We feel safe when we're in control. We want to know what's going to happen. We crave predictability. We over plan and then stress when things don't go our way.

We obsess over details and believe there is only one right way. We are critical of others and micromanage. We have impossibly high standards and want things done in a specific way. We are anxious. We don't trust others. We want to know we can succeed at something before we commit.

It's impossible to control others and situations. The effort is futile. It creates problems in relationships and leads to misery. We must practice acceptance because we can only control ourselves.

Distinguish what's in and what's out of our control. Stop giving unwanted advice. Stop pushing situations to be something they aren't. No one is perfect.

Most fear comes from the thought, "If something happens, I won't be able to handle it." We are capable of handling anything that comes our way. Trust and move on.

Quote: "God grant me the serenity to accept the things I cannot change, the courage to change the things I can and the wisdom to know the difference." – Dr. Reinhold Niebuhr, American Theologian.

Resource: *Faith* by Dr. Joe Vitale

Action Step: When you start controlling, repeat these statements:

- "I can only control myself."
- "My way isn't the only way."
- "I hold others capable."
- Repeat until you calm down.

For years I worked 80+ hours per week. I had trust issues. I was controlling and didn't hold people capable. I didn't trust they could get results and didn't give them a chance to prove themselves. I always believed I could do it better.

The team got my appreciation if they produced and felt my disapproval if they didn't. I wanted them to win, often more than they did. I took it personally if they won or lost.

If they lost, I believed it was a reflection on me, and I was the loser. I was somehow responsible for their failure. I spent significant time trying to fix people. I felt that they needed to be just like me.

I thought I gave great advice, but most didn't take it. I would judge them and take it personally when they didn't do what I wanted them to do. I was stressed, and my relationships were strained. Something had to change.

I needed to release my need to control. I needed to accept people for who they were, not what I wanted them to be. I needed to stop rescuing them. I could continue to help but it was their choice to succeed or fail. I wasn't responsible if they won or lost.

I decided to hold them 100% accountable and capable. I met with my leaders to clarify my new expectations. They appreciated the conversation and valued my willingness to help. However, they were comfortable and didn't want more.

They no longer wanted my help. It had nothing to do with me. I learned to love them anyway. I was only able to control myself. The proverbial piano I had been carrying for years was instantly removed. This was the catalyst for our team's transformation and for me as a leader.

26. Mind The Gap

Relationships fail because of the expectation gap. Our expectations, as well as the expectations of others. We fear having uncomfortable conversations. The longer we wait, the less likely the conversation will ever occur. We believe we're right, and they're wrong. We create unspoken expectations. We don't express it, but we expect people to behave in a certain way.

Unfortunately, people aren't mind readers. They have no idea we resent them for not living up to our standards. We catch them falling short. We resent them, and they don't know why. It hurts the relationship and causes needless suffering that could've been handled in a simple conversation.

Quote: "Sometimes we create our own heartbreak through expectation." – Unknown

Resource: *The Path to Liberty* by Thomas Willhite, Founder of Psi Seminars

Action Step:
1. Choose a situation where you have a gap in expectations.
2. Schedule a meeting.
3. Apologize for not having clear expectations.
4. Agree on what you both want, meet in the middle, and move forward.

My first marriage had a gap. We both had expectations, and mine were mainly unspoken. I didn't like confrontation, so I kept everything to myself. She had no chance because I never told her. I was irritated that she couldn't read my mind, and the marriage failed.

I was repeating the cycle again in my second marriage. My kids from the first marriage were young, and I wanted Marlow to be their second mom, yet I never told her. She wasn't interested. When they were eight and five years old, they visited for 10 days. I was looking for Marlow to behave in a certain way, but it wasn't going well. I was irritated that she wasn't living up to the unspoken standard.

I got sage advice two days into their trip: "Relax, Chris quit creating an unrealistic expectation of her; let it go, let it be." Total gamechanger. I let it go, and the trip was joyful.

Marlow and I had a conversation to close the gap. What did she want? She wanted to enjoy my kids and love them. She wasn't interested in being their mom. They always had a good time together and appreciated each other. She's not a second mom. She helps when they reach out, but it's not often. They already have an amazing mom and support system.

What did I want? Something she didn't. I realized what I wanted wasn't necessary for anyone's happiness. I dropped it. We met in the middle and moved on. No more gap. We now have a full and functional relationship.

27. Stay Together

Great relationships are paramount to happiness. They can bring both joy and heartache. They take time to nurture yet can be ruined in minutes. Tying our happiness to the behavior of another creates problems.

We often want others to change while we insist on staying the same. We will find what we search for. If we look for the negative, we will notice it. The issue gets exacerbated, and everything is viewed from a lens of dysfunction.

Often, we project onto others what we don't like about ourselves. To create successful relationships, we must think loving thoughts and mentally elevate others. We should see them how they want to be seen and focus on the good.

Communicate the good you see. This requires an intentional re-focus as our brain is wired to focus on the negative. You can only change yourself, so keep your focus there.

Lifting others creates chemistry and harmony. Never underestimate the power of positive projection.

Quote: "The Grass is Greener Where you Water it." – Neil Barringham, Author

Resource: AwesomeMarriage.com by Dr. Kim Kimberling

Action Step: Journal:

1. Choose a relationship that isn't working.
2. List the great things you see in this person.
3. Schedule a time to share your list with them.

I had a destructive, unconscious relationship pattern. I would fall in love and incessantly think about them. The newness would wear off, and the excitement would fade. Then, to light the spark, we would fight. I needed to always be right and ended up being easily offended.

We would stay together, but I would start fault-finding. I was perfect, so I didn't need to change, but she sure did. I would start dreaming of that ideal unicorn relationship that was effortless and easy. 'The grass is always greener somewhere else' is a trap.

I would stay to avoid confrontation, but eventually, it would end. I did this with ex-girlfriends as well as my first wife. They had no chance. Even if they were perfect, I would self-sabotage. I'm grateful they got away from me and found the love they deserved.

My second marriage followed the same pattern. We had major financial adversity. I allowed my wife's stress to shift my focus from finding the good to focusing on the bad. If she would only change, then all would be well.

One day, we had the fight of all fights. She exploded, threw her purse, and listed all my shortcomings; she was done. I asked her why we were still married, and the fight stopped immediately. She went upstairs to ponder the question. Thankfully, she spent the time finding reasons to stay.

I was alone with my thoughts and could see the dominoes falling. I created everything. I was the common denominator to all my messes, and I was going down that path again.

I'm married to the woman of my dreams and about to blow it. Thankfully, she focused on my good qualities in her moment of intense emotion. She didn't want to lose those things. Instead, she focused on the good and left the bad behind.

I decided to interrupt my destructive pattern and do the same. The next day, we decided to stay together, avoid bankruptcy and figure it out. Without her, the life we have wouldn't have happened. I thank God every day for her and that we stayed married.

28. Check Your Motives

The masses have a negative view of the sales profession. They have images of a slick and manipulative used car salesman. We've all experienced an unforgettably bad sales situation. Unfortunately, our brains gravitate toward negative experiences and often forget positive sales interactions.

When starting a sales career, many believe they must become someone they're not. They behave inauthentically and believe they need to push and persuade. They use hard closing techniques. Their motives are money and recognition. They focus on themselves instead of the client.

No one wants that experience. In sales, we must focus on the client and listen. People are rarely heard and acknowledged. Listening relaxes the client and decreases resistance. It's not a sales technique but a way to be.

As Shirzad Chamine states in Positive Intelligence. "*Most salespeople agreed that much of their attention was still on themselves and their own concerns during a sales call. They asked themselves questions like, Will I be able to make this sale? How am I doing? Do they like me? When they stop talking, what smart thing can I say? True empathy for someone else means that you place all of your attention on them. When we put ourselves in their shoes and see it from their eyes, it's easier to help them. This is the key to successful selling.*"

To get the sale, we need to stop worrying about making the sale. The successful result occurs when we stop thinking about what's in it for us and solve the client's problem.

Quote: "People don't care how much you know until they know how much you care." – Theodore Roosevelt, 26th U.S. President

Resource: *Positive Intelligence* by Shirzad Chamine

Action Step:

1. Get a Sales Journal.
2. Rate yourself on a scale of 1-10 after each appointment, with 10 being a total focus on the client and 1 with the focus on you.
3. Document what did and didn't work.
4. Where do you need to improve?

We were digging out of our financial hole. I was working hard but ineffectively. I was in a sales slump. I had many meetings, but nothing was closing. I was the best unpaid financial advisor around.

I was operating from lack and need. During a coaching call, I lamented about my closing issues, and his advice transformed my career.

He said, "You're not closing because you have an agenda. You're focused on what you will get out of it. You're focused on the money and your clients sense your neediness. They don't have a good feeling and will never commit. Then you get 'think it overs' and stalls. It must be about them and how they benefit. You're pushing them away. Before the next meeting, write down all the ways they will benefit. Check your motives and clear your agenda."

This was groundbreaking for my career. I arrived 30 minutes early for my next appointment. I sat in my car and wrote down every way my client would benefit. It was a huge list of positives that increased my belief.

This was going to be awesome for them. It took the pressure off. I made it about them. I presented the plan, and they instantly moved forward. The slump was over.

This forever changed how I sold. It took the focus off me and placed it where it should've always been; on my client.

29. Your Need to be Right Will Cost You Your Life

In school, the smart ones get praise and recognition. Parents want smart kids and love bragging about them. It feeds the kid's ego and identity. For those of us who didn't have natural ability, we constructed the facade of being smart.

When kids are taught something, they have a knee-jerk response of "I know that." This is a protective response to cover up a delicate psyche. No one wants to look stupid.

This programming usually goes unchecked and continues into adulthood. People who need to be right have fragile egos. If their self-image is challenged, they make themselves appear smarter and superior. They blame others for their mistakes, and their self-righteous behavior creates issues.

These people are challenging to work with. Their behavior tends to widen the gap between themselves and everyone else. They lose connection with others and push people away. Self-righteous people tend to be hypocritical and unknowingly have a double standard. They offer advice to which they fail to adhere.

How do we feel when someone proves themselves right and us wrong? We feel bad and want to get away. Self-righteousness destroys relationships.

If this describes you, take some time to be introspective and assess the price paid for your behavior. Is it worth it? Make a commitment to personal development and coaching. Get feedback about how you show up. Peace happens with peaceful relationships.

You'll be alone if you don't change, which can be hell on earth. It takes work, but those holes of insecurity can be healed. It's worth it. If someone you love is self-righteous, schedule time to gently make your feelings known. Don't attack, but give them the feedback they need. It could be the turning point that changes everything.

Quote: "Your actions speak so loudly; I can't hear what you are saying." – Ralph Waldo Emerson, American Author.

Resource: *Ego is the Enemy* by Ryan Holiday

Action Step: Journal:

1. How has self-righteous behavior negatively affected you? Journal on a situation.
2. What was the trigger?
3. What was the impact?
4. How has this behavior impacted those closest to you?
5. What work needs to be done?
6. If necessary, hire a coach.

Growing up, I admired smart people. They always seemed to have the answers. They got attention and recognition.

I created an early belief that I wasn't smart. School was hard and I was a slow learner. To understand the content, I needed to read things repeatedly. While many understood things right away, it took me several hours. College was the same. I counteracted this deficiency with desire and work ethic. I put in late nights, but I eventually succeeded.

Then I started my first job. Corporate America was political, and smarts were revered. The smartest guys were elevated. Being self-righteous worked. Winning the argument was a skill. It worked in the corporate world, but as an entrepreneur, this mindset was disastrous.

It was incredibly damaging when building a volunteer team. In my business, they follow you because they want to, not because they must. My need to be right and to look smart pushed people away.

I was winning the battle but losing the war. I was a hypocrite. I wasn't doing what I was telling them to do. It wasn't working.

One day I was arguing with my coach, and he called me out. The fight was useless, but I was triggered, and I wasn't letting go. When emotion goes up, intelligence goes down.

He asked, "Do you want to be right, or do you want to be at peace?"

I wanted peace and had none of it in my life.

Then he stated, "Your need to be right will cost you your life!"

This shook me to the core. He was spot on!

My first marriage had failed because I needed to be right. I had been self-righteous with others in business and my personal life. It wasn't working, and I didn't like the results.

I had to work on my emotional intelligence. I assessed past failures of when I won but ultimately lost. The price I paid was significant. This changed my awareness.

Now, I get prepared when entering a potentially heated situation. I use mental rehearsal to prepare my responses. It keeps my emotions in check and grounded.

I stay present and listen intently. I pray for guidance. I'm not perfect, but I'm better than I used to be. Often, I just let it go. It doesn't mean you become a pushover, as healthy conflict can be beneficial. Sometimes you need to hold your ground, but you can do it in a powerful, peaceful way. We intuitively know when things go from healthy to unhealthy. Don't cross that line. Let them be right.

The older I get, the more I want peace. Being right is overrated.

30. Stop Judging

Judgment is our primary form of self-sabotage. Judging ourselves starts in childhood and develops into adulthood. It's part of our thinking, and we never question it.

We believe what our ego tells us; usually, it's a negative dialogue. As a result, we can never live up to the standard it holds.

We would never talk to others the way we speak to ourselves. Judging ourselves is universal. It's a destructive pattern, and we're not alone. Most everyone suffers and feels inadequate, undeserving, and guilty.

We also judge others and find qualities in others that we don't like about ourselves. It's called projection. One finger pointed out, and three fingers pointed back. Everything we see in another; we strengthen in ourselves.

Negative thoughts towards others are more about ourselves, not them. It robs us of joy and peace. Judgment creates issues with our relationships, health, and finances. The worst part about judgment is it's often delusional. Our lives can be consumed with the lie of judgment, and it's tragic.

The good news is we can change, and self-awareness is the solution. It begins with recognizing how we feel. When we feel bad, we are probably judging. It's then necessary to shift our thoughts to stop fighting ourselves.

Break the thought pattern by reciting an affirmation or scripture. Journal the story you're making up. To help release the attachment, there are many technologies available. Invest in these programs and use them.

Start focusing on the good you see in others and document their positive traits. Review often and re-affirm. Your view of them will change, and it will transform the relationship.

It takes energy to achieve our goals and dreams. Judgment of self and others is the biggest energy leak that exists. It is the path to failure.

Quote: "The world is a great mirror. It reflects back to you what you are." – Thomas Dreier, American Editor.

Resource: www.centerpointe.com Holosync Meditation.

www.learningstrategies.com , Paraliminals, Personal Development for busy people.

These are transformational technologies, invest in them.

Action Step: Intently study judgment. Get *Positive Intelligence* by Shirzad Chamine. Complete the exercises in the book. www.positiveintelligence.com

I constantly judged myself and others. My brain was a busy place with ongoing chatter. It's a miracle I accomplished anything. My thinking was consumed by judgment. Judging and beating myself up and judging others for not fulfilling my expectations. Judging people more successful than me. Judging my less-than-desirable environment. I was in a constant state of dissatisfaction, albeit I could put a smile on my face and fake it.

I had to stop being a hypnotic robot, so I went all-in on my personal development. I learned that I could control my thinking. This was groundbreaking, as I never thought it was possible. I wanted to be a high achiever and feel peace.

This wouldn't happen by chance, so I needed to invest the time to change. I wanted a quiet brain, free from chatter and judgment. This became an obsession.

A peaceful mind equals a peaceful world. I was being judged a lot. Like a boomerang, all my judgment returned to me. I wanted less strife in my relationships. I studied, meditated, and invested in powerful technologies to quiet my mind. After a few months, I was changing. I was rewiring my mind and creating peace. I left overwhelm and stress behind. I still had problems but was no longer emotionally attached to them. I had internal peace for the first time and was able to focus.

With a quiet mind, I focused on my judgment issues. I became aware of when I judged myself and others. I would interrupt the thought pattern with a simple "stop" and redirect to a positive affirmation or scripture. Habitual thinking takes time to change, but I was determined to shift.

If I wanted love, I needed to send out more loving thoughts. It wasn't quick, but I eventually got better. It's still a project for me, but I'm hyper aware when judgmental thoughts occur. It's so damaging, and I must stop it before it progresses.

People are stressed because of mind chatter and judgment. I recommend coaches, tools, and technologies to help, and I'm surprised when people don't act. Their judgment is keeping them stuck. You won't find peace if you can't control your thinking. Get to work. You'll be glad you did.

31. Be a Spark

We want our lives to count. We want significance, which only comes through helping others. We have our goals, dreams, fears, and worries. It's easy to make it about ourselves.

When we succeed, it's due to the countless people who helped us. Our parents, teachers, coaches, friends, family, and teammates who shared their wisdom and guidance. They cared for and believed in us. Being successful is a team event, and we can't do it on our own. We are forever grateful for these people and want to be that for others.

Growing ourselves is a must. The more valuable we become, the more value we can share. Our challenges are lessons for others. However, it's easy to hold ourselves back and buy the lies of our ego. We aren't the example yet. We don't know enough and aren't good enough.

What will they think of me? Our limited view of ourselves gets in the way. We don't see ourselves as being valuable. We get an intuitive insight to share and then stop ourselves. We get ready to get ready.

You do have value and insight to share. People are stuck in their thinking, and sometimes we just need to be a spark. We don't need to be some powerful almighty leader. Listening and asking a question could be the spark they need. It could shift their dysfunctional paradigm and create a new perspective.

Just listening could allow someone to verbalize and reach their own conclusions. We don't need to do it for them, and we don't need to rescue anyone. We don't need to be perfect. We just need to care and share. We could be the spark that starts the blaze.

Our success is great, but its fulfillment is limited. Our impact on others is where the juice is. You're qualified to do it. Wanting to help and caring is all that is needed. You could be the spark that makes all the difference.

Quote: "The smallest spark can become the greatest light." – George E. Miller, Artist.

Resource: *Infinite Possibilities* by Mike Dooley

Action Step: Set the intention to listen more and talk less today. Listen intently to what the other person is saying and pay attention to any intuitive insight that could help. Share it with them. Don't hold back.

I was in Atlanta visiting my kids. Our company's headquarters was 40 minutes from where I was staying. I received a call from one of the company executives asking if I was in town. Their closing speaker for a leadership academy couldn't make it. I needed to step in. For a few hours, I shared my story and lessons.

You never know how you can impact others. This is a story from one of those participants:

"I was at the lowest point of my life. Son of immigrant parents, husband, father to a beautiful daughter, a broke N.Y.C. Brooklyn boy with big dreams. Our money problems created marriage problems. We were convinced that separation was the only solution.

My wife went with me to a leadership academy for which I qualified. She agreed to go to support me, even though we weren't staying together. The last speaker shared his struggle and how he survived his marriage storm. What he shared was the answer to my prayers. It was the compass to exit the darkest moment of my life. He enlightened us on how to create change.

It's about doing things in a certain way. He talked about setting goals that seemed impossible and how to get out of our own way. For example, I was only making a few thousand per month, which was not enough to survive in New York City. I wanted to make $25,000 per month.

I tried many times. I had the plan but always found a way to self-sabotage. I was consumed with fear, doubt, and worry. He shared how to avoid all the noise, doubt, and fear. He taught us the "What if" concept. "What if I can?" "What if" laid the foundation for hope, created possibilities, and removed all doubt. Wow, I could literally If my way to success.

I reiterated to my wife that "what if" was our key to changing everything. What if I can make $25,000 next month?

Lessons are caught, not taught, and I caught it.

I 'what if'd' in the cab drive to the airport, on the airplane, in the shower, eating meals. What if we could make $25,000 in April? What would my life look like? What would change? I was obsessed. For the next six months, I was 'what if'ing' constantly.

My wife thought I was going crazy, but I was enjoying it. I finished April at $26,000, and the following month I made $23,000. A colleague asked what was different. I told him, "I'm if-ing my way to success." He challenged me to "if" my way to $50,000 the following month. I surpassed it with $54,000.

In the shower, I reflected on the magical last 90 days. I was so grateful as I went from the abyss to making $100,000 in 3 months. Then intuition hit. WHAT IF WE CAN SAVE $100,000? I got fired up and told my wife that we needed to open a bank account immediately. She was surprised. We didn't have a bank account together as she didn't want a joint account with a broke person.

The goal was to save $100,000 in six months. She asked how I said, "What if we can?" By December, we saved $100,000. For the next six months, we did it again, then again, then again. My thoughts created tremendous momentum. The 'What if' system changed everything. It was like the moment when Spider-Man discovered he had webs.

Here's my observation.

The answer to your prayers, goals, and dreams has always been, still is, and will forever be a person. Everything you have ever gotten that you're proud of, someone helped you get it.

Stop looking for the thing and start being open to the person. What you want will never appear in your life as a thing; it will appear to you in the form of a person. The person helps you get the thing you need the most.

This simple concept transformed my world. It was the spark that created the fire that saved my business, marriage, and family, and I'm forever grateful.

32. Keep Your Word

There are many goals to set and plans to be made. However, make keeping your word a top priority. Integrity is doing what you say you will do. For most people, this concept has lost relevance.

People who struggle don't keep their word and fail to deliver on their commitments. "Excusitis" is a national pastime. Blaming, justifications, and validations are everywhere. High divorce rates. Soaring personal debt. Out of control spending. Small businesses are failing.

The root of failure begins small. Blowing things off, not finishing, being late, ghosting people, missing appointments, and little white lies. Everyone else does it, so it must be okay. The ripple effect is profound.

Our addiction to comfort leads to only doing things that feel good. It erodes our confidence. We believe we can't be trusted. If we can't trust ourselves, why go after our dreams? We stay stuck. This root issue creates stress and dysfunction. It's a huge price to pay.

Clean it up. If you don't keep your word, be the first to admit it. Don't wait for someone to hold you accountable. Show up, be early, follow up and finish. If you can't deliver, don't hide. Admit it and own it. People are always looking for the secret sauce for success. Focus here; it will transform your world.

Quote: "You should always keep your word. All the setbacks in life come only because you don't keep your word." – Sivananda, Hindu Spiritual Teacher.

Resource: The Four Agreements by Don Miguel Ruiz

Action Step: Make a decision:

1. Make keeping your word a top priority.
2. In your morning routine, scan your calendar and affirm, "I'm keeping my word today."
3. At night, rate yourself on a scale of 1-10.
4. How did you do with keeping your word that day?
5. What change can you make to improve for tomorrow?

It was the beginning of a four-day seminar. On a scale of 1-10, I was asked to rate myself on keeping my word. I was excited as my delusional thinking was, "I got this one nailed." I'm definitely a 9 out of 10. I always do what I say I'm going to do. I never break promises to myself or others.

We were given instructions and rules throughout the four days, which we agreed to. At the end, we rehashed the rules and were asked about our follow-through. I thought I had listened well, but no. Some of the things they mentioned I didn't remember and several I blew off. The rules I followed were items that I felt like doing.

The reassessment on keeping my word; 3 out of 10. The feedback was valuable, as I did this seminar like I did my life. I stunk at keeping my word and was delusional in my assessment.

It was difficult, but I reflected on the impact of not keeping my word. I didn't keep my word in my first marriage, and I was doing the same in the second one. I didn't even keep my word to my kids. As a result, my business was suffering. Broken promises to myself. My health wasn't good. I avoided the uncomfortable things that were necessary to succeed. I was broke and in debt. Not keeping my word impacted every area of my life.

I woke up and realized the heavy price everyone was paying, including me. This had to change. It was difficult to look at, but I eventually forgave myself. I was energized because if I could clean this up, it would unlock the door to success.

This became a primary focus. Keeping small promises to myself and others created momentum, and keeping the bigger promises became easier. I stopped overcommitting and said no to things on which I couldn't deliver. If I didn't keep my word, I stopped making excuses. I owned it. Keeping my word released guilt, and this increased my confidence and energy. It allowed others to trust me.

My results drastically improved by focusing on this simple concept. I'm not perfect, but way better than I used to be. It has paid big dividends. When I coach people, I start here. They want to focus on many things, but those who fail don't keep their word. Focus here, and the rest takes care of itself.

33. Be a Giver

We've heard that it's better to give than to receive. We want to help, but we get in our own way. Giving is an afterthought. Once our needs are met, then we can help others. The focus is on us.

One day I'll get around to giving. How can I get what I want first? When our energy is being expended to get, there isn't much left to give.

Takers are all about self-interest and manipulation. They believe their lives will be the total of what they get. They might get what they want, but it doesn't end well. They try to fill a void that can't be filled. The peace for which they yearn evades them.

Another group is in the middle. They give but immediately look for a return. They keep score and give in a manipulative way. A gift with an ulterior motive is not a gift; it's a bribe. It's self-serving. This creates a mediocre existence.

There are 100% Givers, who have weak receiving muscles. They give all the time and can become doormats. Some don't believe they deserve love or success, which doesn't end well. They eventually hit the wall with nothing left to give, become susceptible to burnout, and become bitter.

In nature, giving and receiving are effortless. Bees feed on the nectar of the flower, and the flower relies on the bees to cross-pollinate. It's natural. Giving and receiving should be as well.

True giving is a selfless act minus any expectation of reciprocity. The key to successful giving is to allow it to occur naturally. Never force it. It's not a sacrifice to give. Unfortunately, many believe that giving reduces their energy to receive. They don't believe they will benefit from giving, so it's not worth the effort.

When we give to others, fear disappears. We are energized. When we are giving, our personal anxieties dissipate. Please recognize that the best interest of another is in our own best interest. We experience peace and freedom from conflict.

When people with a disease help another in a similar place, they detach from their own symptoms and helplessness. They feel relief.

Set the intention today to first add value. You will find what you are looking for. Stop worrying about the return and how you will benefit. The law is exact. If you work in a giving consciousness, you must receive. Trust it and take the first step. How can you give today?

Quote: "Discover the wonder of giving. It is the better way. And the day will come when you insist it is the only way" – Eric Butterworth, Author.

Resource: *Prosperity* by Charles Fillmore

Action Step: Be intentional.

1. Every morning, set the giving intention.
2. Scan your calendar and see where you can add value.
3. Be open to new opportunities.
4. Set the intention before every meeting.
5. How can I serve this person?
6. Pay attention to intuitive answers and act.

I was in the middle of my personal crisis. Searching for answers, I attended a 7-day seminar. The seminar's purpose was to provide feedback, which I hated. I was delusional. I thought I was awesome and spent time proving it to myself and others, so I didn't need feedback.

However, there was a disconnect between my awesomeness and my pathetic results. Finally, after 3 days of getting to know the other participants, we did an exercise that changed everything.

We were given a blank sheet of paper. In the top left corner, we wrote "Giver," and in the opposite corner, "Taker." We lined up, and people cycled through. We took a second to tell each person how they were viewed as givers or takers. Each participant gave and received feedback.

As a receiver, we kept score by noting each response. I wasn't ready for this intense level of feedback. My ego didn't like it. I resented those who called me a taker. They were obviously clueless, and I reciprocated by labeling them as takers.

In the end, we tallied the total for the giver and taker. We were ranked from #1, the one with the most giver responses, to last, the one with the most taker responses. I was in the middle of the pack. I was shocked as this didn't line up with my inflated ego, yet, it was consistent with my middle-of-the-pack results. I gave only out of self-interest.

I intently observed the guy who was last. The biggest taker in the room. He was a good guy and didn't fit my idea of a taker. He wasn't mean or arrogant, but he kept to himself. He didn't contribute at all. I never connected a taker as someone that didn't contribute. He stayed in his comfort zone.

This experience transformed him. After the seminar, we stayed in contact, and he thrived. Without this feedback, he would've never known. Instead, he would've stayed in his dysfunctional comfort zone and lived an unfulfilled life.

We don't like feedback, but the initial sting leads to change if received correctly. I needed feedback. At that point in my life, I was a taker, and this needed to change.

My weekly game plan now includes a giving component. I can always improve, but I'm better than I used to be. In the morning, I ask how I can add value that day. I need reminders to serve others. Otherwise, it's easy to make it about me.

Before every meeting, I ask for guidance on how to serve. It's an infinite game to keep the focus on others, but it's worth it. Service to others is the juice of life. Even though the feedback hurt, it was necessary. I'm grateful that I embraced it and improved instead of discounting it.

Pillar 4

The Game Plan

34. Know Your A & B

A successful journey requires knowing where you are (point A) and where you're going (Point B). Your G.P.S. system guides you based on these 2 points. If you don't know A and B, your G.P.S. is useless.

In sailing, the captain plots his points, pulls the anchor, and leaves the dock. He constantly adjusts the sails based on the weather. The focus is on the first stop and then the next.

This also applies to goal setting. We often look at point B with overwhelm. The trap lies in attempting to calculate the entire journey. Too many variables exist. We experience "paralysis by analysis" and never leave. Our only job is to define point B. Then start the journey, get feedback, and adjust the sails. These small course corrections keep us on track.

Quote: "If you don't know where you are going, any road will get you there." – Lewis Carroll, English Author

Resource: *The Power of Intention* by Dr. Wayne Dyer

Action Step: Journal:

1. What is your #1 goal?
2. Define points A and B.
3. Identify your first step and take it.
4. Then focus on the next.

During a seminar exercise, we were given a map of a 2,000-acre ranch. We were instructed to find point A on the map. Point B was highlighted. The goal was to locate B to camp for the night. My group of 10 men had no map skills. We guessed point A and started the journey. Eight hours later, we were lost, walking in circles in the dark. It was only a 2-hour trek. Finally, we were rescued and guided to camp.

I reflected and noted my thinking during the 8-hour debacle. I did this exercise like I did my life. "I will eventually get there. I just need to grind, persist, and keep moving even if it takes all night. One day I will be successful."

I was pushing my success off one more day. These mind viruses seemed harmless, yet they were damaging. They were stopping me from ever getting to point B. I was casual and didn't know where I was or where I was going. I couldn't continue to kill myself and never reach my destination. Something had to change.

After this seminar, I changed my goal-setting process. I committed to always knowing my A and B and making weekly small course corrections along the way. This single strategy catapulted my success.

35. Get a Coach

Success is practically impossible without coaching. Going it alone leads to failure at worst and mediocrity at best. Our pride leads us to believe that we have all the answers. To avoid looking weak, we don't ask for help.

A coach guides us. They help us avoid mistakes and duplicate successful strategies. Engage a coach who has achieved the desired results and respect his or her time. Be intentional and prepared. What are the keys to success? Where are you stuck? How can he or she help?

Don't force the coach to pull the information from you; glean what you need from him or her. Don't be casual. Avoid telling stories and get to the point. No excuses for your lack of performance. You either did it, or you didn't. Take 100% responsibility for your results.

Victims can't be coached, and they never succeed. Be focused. No multitasking during coaching sessions. Do what he or she tells you to do. Don't be selectively coachable by doing what's comfortable. Don't take instruction and then shop opinions with others to justify not taking their advice. If you don't trust him or her, get another coach. Implement at the speed of instruction. There is only one way to reward your coach and get more time. Be 100% coachable and follow through.

Quote: "A coach is someone who can give correction without causing resentment." – John Wooden.

Resource: *Three Feet from Gold* by Sharon L. Lechter & Dr. Greg S. Reid

Action Step: Prepare for your next mentoring session.

1. What did you say you were going to do?
2. Did you do it? Yes or No. No stories.
3. If not, what became more important than keeping your word?
4. What did you learn?
5. What is going to be different moving forward?

I was at my lowest point. I was staring at massive debt, negative cash flow, and a stressed-out wife. My kids were on the other side of the country, wondering where Dad was. I couldn't work any harder. My energy was zapped, and I was burned out. My confidence was low, and I saw no way out. The harder I worked, the deeper I sunk.

Against my pride, I hired a coach with money I didn't have. I tried to self-sabotage. I no-showed our first coaching session as my ego couldn't handle the truth. Thankfully, he stayed. He saw something in me that I didn't see anymore.

Our first few sessions were useless. I didn't know if I could trust him. I was guarded and wasted time trying to get his approval. I tried impressing him with my brilliance. I was justifying my lack of success, and I was delusional. I tried to convince him that it wasn't that bad. Optimism and delusion sleep in the same bed together.

My focus was an impossible savings goal that was imperative to Marlow. During a call, he asked if we had saved any money the prior week. I said, "Coach, we didn't save because we didn't have any money to save." He responded, "You've been using that excuse for years; how much longer are you going to use it? You need to save money!" My arrogant response was, "I know that." He became angry. If we were in person, he would've punched me.

The following instruction transformed my life. He said, "Don't ever say that again. Based on results, you don't know $&@! # squat. You're broke and miserable. Your wife won't take this much longer. You don't know anything. If you say 'I know that' again this coaching relationship is over. I'll know you know when you're living the results."

"I know it" is a dangerous trap. We dismiss the instruction, refuse to change, and stay stuck. He woke me up, and I never said it again. I didn't want to hear this, but I needed it. I was an expert at fooling people and couldn't do it anymore. I went all in on his coaching. I respected his time and did everything he told me to do. I was trusting and vulnerable. Eventually, I hit all my goals. I paid him back with my results.

36. Get It Together

Casual people become casualties. The masses are casual about their lives. Most are aimless and addicted to comfort. They spend more time planning their vacations than they do their lives. They don't value their time because they believe it's unlimited. They are superstitious and often count on luck and chance. They believe success is outside their control. They don't plan as they believe it won't matter.

We live in the richest country, yet most people retire broke. Very few small businesses survive, let alone thrive. The masses are distracted, and their habits don't serve them. This creates problems with their health, relationships, and money. They wake up, and their thoughts are dictated by what happens. The outside world is always unstable, so their thinking and results match.

They aren't intentional and leave things to chance. They operate based on habitual patterns of the past. When you ask them how they are, their knee-jerk response is, "I'm busy." Very true. Busy but getting nowhere. Their thinking and lack of preparation create stress and chaos. Running on a hamster wheel is no way to live. If don't prepare to thrive, you will just survive.

To create the life you want, you must plan. This time is allocated to think and plan your life. Keep the appointment with yourself, and don't schedule over it. This process creates clarity of thinking. It removes the stress and chaos from your life.

There are still issues outside your control, but you will have the focus to handle them. It sends a message that you have it together and can be trusted. Begin this habit; it will transform your life and create the desired results.

Quote: "If you fail to plan, you are planning to fail." – Benjamin Franklin, Founding Father of the U.S.A.

Resource: https://amzn.to/3Bru8gt Planner Pad 2023

Action Step: Schedule planning time in your calendar. Sometime between Friday afternoon and Sunday. Plan until you feel you're 100% ready for the week.

I learned a lot from my dad. He was the best salesperson I've ever seen. He had great energy and made instant connections with people. A charismatic dreamer with an amazing work ethic. Still, he would have momentum and then fail. In the end, he had the talent to succeed, but it never happened.

I learned a major lesson. The line between winning and losing is extremely thin. To succeed, you can't leave anything to chance.

I committed to being prepared. I never took opportunities for granted. I controlled what I could control. People die the death of a thousand cuts, but that wasn't going to be me. I would have wins and losses, but lack of preparation would never be an issue.

I scheduled time to plan, set weekly goals, and reviewed results. Then, I made course corrections and planned my week. I believe one hour of planning saves eight hours. I planned until I got the internal feeling that I was 100% ready for the week. Then, I started the week with confidence and focus. I was like a football coach with his game plan.

I'm amazed at how many entrepreneurs don't prepare. They start their week with no plan or intention. They suffer from intention deficit disorder and ultimately fail when it could've been avoided.

Take the time to plan. It's work, not fun. But you can schedule fun because you're not wasting time. You can get great results and have fun at the same time. It's worth it. Get It Together.

37. Don't Eat the Elephant

We are told to think big, go big or go home. We set a BHAG (Big, Hairy, Audacious Goal). Our initial excitement turns into fear while standing at base camp looking up at Mt. Everest. Our fight or flight response is triggered, and we feel overwhelmed. We attempt to navigate the entire climb. It seems impossible, so we procrastinate. We distract ourselves and never start. Until the next time, when we are told to think big, go big... the cycle repeats with the same result.

To avoid this, we need to think small. It doesn't work when we try to eat the whole elephant in one bite. Set the big goal, get excited, and understand that the journey starts with the first step. Focus on getting to Base Camp One. The first action should lead to this conclusion: "I can do that."

In sales, don't make 50 calls; make one. A body in motion stays in motion. The momentum of the first call will lead to the second. Don't tackle the whole workout; put your shoes on and get moving. Just floss one tooth.

Small steps bypass our fight-or-flight response. Small steps don't create overwhelm. Your focus is on the next step, not the whole mountain. The compounding of small steps is powerful. Successful people take small steps and create huge success. The masses discount it, struggle and never start. Apply it. It will change your life.

Quote: "A Journey of a thousand miles begins with a single step." – Lao Tzu, Chinese Philosopher.

Resource: *One Small Step Can Change Your Life: The Kaizen Way* by Dr. Robert Mauer

Action Step: Journal:

1. What is your #1 goal?
2. What's the first "I can do that" step you need to take?

Broke and in massive debt, Marlow and I set our first couple's goal; save $100k. If we couldn't save money, we would never be financially free. It shifted my focus to creating wealth versus fixing the debt. However, the goal seemed impossible with $250k in unsecured debt and no savings.

My mind started racing with paralyzing thoughts: "How will it happen? It's too far away. You haven't saved before, how's this going to be different?"

We had to chunk it down to bypass the overwhelm and start small. Eat the elephant in smaller bites. We focused on saving the first $10k. I created a mental movie. Marlow loved to ski; it was her getaway and release. I visualized her coming down the stairs mid-week in her ski outfit, kissing me, and going skiing.

I attached that experience to our first $10k saved. I would end that 5-minute visualization in tears as the first $10k symbolized relief. It meant she felt financially secure enough to take the day off. This planted seeds in my subconscious mind and changed my savings habits.

As a result, I eliminated all wasted expenditures. Small dollars led to bigger dollars, and the habit was forming. We hit that first goal, and it felt amazing. If we could save $10k, we could save $25k, and so on.

The small step focus created forward momentum. The snowball turned into an avalanche of success. We continue to set big goals but always focus on the first step.

38. Work Hard but Don't Make Hard Work of It

We were programmed during childhood that life is tough, and success is hard. We embark on a "hero's journey" where we believe we must overcome and have our "Rocky" moment to deserve success. Statues aren't erected in our image without the harrowing story of overcoming the odds. Discipline is the key to freedom, and we must have a world-class work ethic. Obstacles will appear.

Start asking yourself, "What if it was easy?"

Will it always be easy? No. However, many self-development gurus insist that everything is hard and you must always grind. I tried this, and it almost killed me. However, the gurus are right, too, because "hard" is what they expect and receive.

Periodically ask yourself, am I making this harder than it should be?

It causes you to think as opposed to just operating from habit. You will find simple solutions to release resistance and increase energy. You will eliminate wasted time. Often people work more than necessary to prove to others that they are "grinding." You will get things done in the time allotted. You'll enjoy the journey and increase results.

Quote: "There's no happy ending to an unhappy journey." – Esther Hicks, Author, Speaker

Resource: *You Squared* by Price Pritchett

Action Step: Ask yourself today at least once, where am I making this harder than it needs to be? Is there a simpler, more efficient way to get the desired result?

My dad taught me that life is hard. He had an amazing work ethic that I adopted. However, his life was hard until he passed at 88 years old. He got what he expected. I accepted "hard" at a young age and never questioned it. I bought into the Hero's Journey and unconsciously created obstacles to overcome.

My hero's journey contributed to my divorce. It led to significant money problems. I worked 80+ hours a week to prove I was a grinder. I was burned out and couldn't keep it up. I started asking myself, what if it were easy? This became a mantra and didn't create bad habits or laziness. Instead, it forced me to think and interrupted my "hard work" program, which usually caused inefficiencies.

The "must work hard" program served me until it didn't. I chose a different thought pattern. It didn't have to be long, arduous, and difficult. I still had challenges but had more energy to handle them. It made me think which is the hardest work of all. This allowed me to eliminate wasted hours and significantly increase my income. I had more fun and stopped worrying about obstacles that hadn't arrived.

39. It's a Project, Not a Problem

Words are powerful. We should only verbalize what we want. Problems are viewed negatively, especially when dealing with impossible situations and difficult people.

From Eric Butterworth in Spiritual Economics, *"When facing a challenge, the better word is "project." Saying "I have this project" makes all the difference. Project suggests a positive endeavor or development. We use tension and strain when dealing with problems. We have a "only a miracle can save me now" consciousness. We tackle a project with vigor and imagination. We believe it can be done."*

If we make a list of problems, we feel terrible, but a list of projects is exciting. We tackle projects with enthusiasm and are eager to start. Problems are static and burdensome, and we feel resentment and self-pity. We often look outside ourselves for a solution. With projects, it's an opportunity to grow. The answers are within.

It's the same so-called "trouble," but our attitude differs. With problems, we stop when faced with a roadblock. We lack conviction and doubt that anything can change. As a result, problems tend to linger and never get handled. With a project, we persist. We become resourceful, acquire skills, and work until it's done.

It doesn't matter how long it takes; eventually, it gets completed. Begin reframing any problems into projects and notice how you feel. Your energy and confidence will increase.

Quote: "There are no problems, only projects." – David Allen, Author

Resource: *Spiritual Economics* by Eric Butterworth

Action Step: Journal:

1. Make a list of lingering problems.
2. Mentally reframe them as projects.
3. Pick one project and write the top three steps you will take today to move the project forward.

At my lowest point, I decided to hire a coach. Based on results, my way wasn't working, yet I was doubtful anyone could help me. I did an initial interview with a coach that lasted two hours. He let me vent, and I whined about everything. I was comparing myself to others. I had a great victim story.

I kept repeating, "I don't know why I'm here; I don't know why I'm not further; I don't know why I'm stuck." Finally, he would ask, "Are you done yet?" I continued, and then the pity party finally ended.

What he said next changed the direction of my life. "Chris, we won't discuss your problems or the past again. We are done with that. Stop justifying your lack of results. You put yourself here, no one else. The only two relevant questions to ask are, 'What do I want?' and 'What is the next thing I need to do?'

You don't have a problem; you have a project. Quit vocalizing problems; it keeps them alive and growing. Your life currently is like an hourglass with black sand. Focus on dropping a little piece of gold in that hourglass every day.

Move your project forward daily. The gold represents the following: getting outside your comfort zone, serving others, contributing, keeping your word, and following up. All these habits will lead to your desired destination. Drop a piece of gold in daily, and before long, the gold will outweigh the black.

That image gave me hope and changed my paradigm. I felt relief for the first time in years. We talked some more, and then he asked, "What are you going to do for the next hour to change your life?" That's when I hired him. That's exactly what I needed. He got me focused on the project and the next step. It wasn't overnight, but everything I dreamed of eventually came true.

40. Grow Up, Be Accountable

When I was growing up, making mistakes was embarrassing. Mistakes were bad and failure was worse. It seemed successful people rarely failed. If we failed, there was something wrong with us. It felt horrible.

Accountability happened when we did something wrong. We were in trouble and punished. These early memories hardened into beliefs about accountability. It's us versus them, and we need to protect ourselves.

This carried into adulthood where we experienced a negative accountability experience. There was an axe to grind. It was done out of spite and caused psychological damage. As a result, we view all accountability from this lens and never step up. We fear being seen as a failure. Being called out surfaces the worst beliefs we have about ourselves. We avoid accountability like the plague.

However, lack of accountability negatively impacts our results. We don't need to love it, but we must stop hating it.

We can't coach ourselves because left to our own devices, we take the easy route. We don't want to feel bad about ourselves, so we never face the music. Instead, we choose distraction and comfort.

Meanwhile, we aren't growing, and our lives are stagnant. We aren't happy because we know we could be doing better. There is dissatisfaction running beneath the surface.

To change results, we need to change, and that doesn't happen on our own. If we knew how to be successful, we already would be. We must commit to change and have a guide that has done it. To achieve the goal, accountability is a must. Otherwise, we take the chicken exit and hide until there is a better time. That time never comes.

Find someone you trust who is where you want to be and reframe your view of accountability. It's the tool needed to achieve the life you want. Take the feedback, put the hammer away that you use on yourself. Be emotionally neutral and implement his or her coaching. Grow up and embrace it.

Quote: "Accountability is the glue that ties commitment to the result." – Bob Proctor, Author

Resource: *The One Minute Millionaire* by Mark Victor Hansen

Action Step: Reach out to a mentor you trust who has achieved your desired results. Schedule a weekly accountability session with them.

As a recovering approval addict, accountability was a downer to my addiction. I did what most do. I would publicly state my goal even though I wasn't committed to it. I promised I was going to do whatever it took to succeed. But deep down, I only hoped it would happen.

I would start slow, hit speed bumps, and conclude I wouldn't succeed. I would give up, go hide and promise to do better next time. I avoided accountability. I took it personally and didn't want to feel bad about myself.

When you don't want to feel bad, you don't want to look. If you have no relationship to results, things get worse. That was me.

Avoiding accountability created personal and financial issues. I had a dysfunctional relationship with accountability.

With a new coach, accountability wasn't optional. He reframed accountability for me. "Chris, it's not about going to the principal's office. I'm not mad at you and you're not in trouble. You need to graduate 5th grade on accountability. Could you imagine repeating 5th grade over and over again? You keep flunking accountability and it's ruining your life, so let's get out of 5th grade."

Accountability was about moving me forward for my reasons and reminding me of my commitments. We all need reminders and coaching to see our blind spots. We need to be hugged and sometimes kicked. It was all done out of love. Without this lesson, I would've failed miserably. There was much on the line for me and my family. Left to myself, I would've continued failing. Without accountability, success would've escaped me. I'm glad I finally graduated.

41. You Can Change, Do the Work

The masses have a fixed mindset. They don't believe they can change. When faced with a challenge, their past dictates their response by default. Limiting beliefs dominate their thinking. "I've never been good at that. If I'm not good at something, I'll never be good at it."

There's no chance for improvement. They avoid the challenge. Instead of growing, they seek comfort and stay stuck. They want to look smart and hope to never be challenged.

Growing requires mental resistance, which doesn't feel good. Most avoid it. Eventually, the masses get fed up with their lives and set a goal, yet they easily quit when challenged. They retreat and back down. Their confidence is damaged, and it hurts. They shrink and buy the lie that they can't change. They believe they are destined to be average. They don't think the effort is worth it, so they stop trying. They live a mediocre existence, haunted by past failures. It's a horrible feeling, so they escape into a world of distractions.

We can change because our brains are constantly evolving. Like a computer, the software can be updated. Your mind is a muscle and can be developed. However, to grow a muscle, it must meet resistance.

You must be intentional about growing and recognize that small efforts compound over time. You shower, eat and brush your teeth daily. You hopefully work out several times a week. You must visit the mental gym every day. This is your daily, uninterrupted, personal development time, preferably in the morning. You spend time alone, work on your vision, meditate, pray, read, and journal.

As you grow, it positively impacts everyone around you. You either grow or decay and there is no middle ground. You're in decay mode if you're not intentional about your growth. That's no way to live. Go to the mental gym daily. It's worth every second.

Quote: "A great life does not happen by accident." – Jonathan Manske, Author, Speaker, and Coach

Resource: *The Miracle Morning: The Not-so-obvious Secret Guaranteed to Transform your Life Before 8am* by Hal Elrod

International Personal Develop Association - Spreading the message of personal development to promote positive change around the world.

Action Step: Journal:
1. What is your plan to grow?
2. Develop your morning routine.
3. Carve out at least 30 minutes to work on your vision, pray, read, meditate, and journal. This is a non-negotiable time.
4. Stick with it.

When I launched my entrepreneurial business, I was frustrated. I thought highly of myself and expected that everything would be sunshine, lollipops, and roses. It was far from that. I was repeatedly hitting the brick wall. I wasn't growing or taking the hint.

Finally, I received sage advice. My current self wasn't the person that was going to hit the goal. I had to grow. I finally accepted it. Then I tried fixing everything at once, and nothing changed. I believed that once I fixed myself, I could move forward. Which could take a lifetime.

Something had to change, so I developed a personal growth plan. I started a daily discipline of going to the mental gym. After this, I needed to execute my plan whether I was ready or not. Even just 30 minutes per day in the mental gym was effective. It equates to 4 ½ working weeks of personal growth per year. Compounded over decades, it's transformational and you will grow.

This habit became my lynchpin for success. The sign of a good habit is if you don't do it, you don't feel well. I must do it. My daily plan includes visualization, Bible reading, and other personal development books. I read my plan aloud, tied to my #1 goal. I also include gratitude, prayer, and dialing in my intention for the day. I end it by answering these 3 questions: How can I grow? What can I give? What can I celebrate? These questions pre-pave my daily mentality and create amazing results.

I benefit, but most importantly, it helps others around me. I can add more value, which is where the joy is. I visit with entrepreneurs who are frustrated with being stuck. These are amazing people who deserve a great life. My message is the same. They must be intentional about growing.

Those who are open to feedback get the same message. Your results haven't changed because you haven't changed. They've aged, but everything is the same. Growth must be intentional and focused.

This small step is life-altering.

42. Respect Money

Broke people disrespect their money. They're careless with even small amounts, which creates large problems. They blow money on frivolous things while indebted to others. They borrow money, hoping things will improve, and the failure cycle continues. They fail to understand that their issue is internal, not external.

Respecting money is imperative to financial success. You and your money are in a relationship, and your bank account reflects its health. Disrespectful attitudes create dysfunctional relationships.

Acquiring wealth is hard work, and that effort deserves respect. Those who prosper treat money respectfully, while those who don't, struggle. Your level of respect for money is directly correlated to the effort expended to acquire it.

Quote: "You must respect people and you must respect money. When you respect money, money will respect you." – Yaya Toure, Professional Soccer Coach and Player.

Resource: *Your Money or Your Life* by Vicki Robin
Secrets of a Millionaire Mind by T. Harv Eker
Couples Money by Marlow & Chris Felton

Action Step: Journal:

    1. Write down ways you have been disrespectful with your money and others.

    2. What problems has this created?

    3. What small step can you take to shift this?

As a kid, we were inundated with money messages like, "Money won't make you happy," "Rich people are crooks," and "You can't take it with you!"

No wonder we struggled with money.

I rarely spent money on big items. It was the small things like eating out, drinks, and coffee. I was dying the financial death of a thousand cuts. I had a mind virus. If I had a bad day, I treated myself. If I had a good day, I celebrated.

I was waiting for a financial windfall to occur before I got it together. I figured I'd track my money once my business started growing. Success is all about small things cared for. If I couldn't be trusted with small dollars, I would never experience the big dollars.

Time to grow up.

I stopped eating out every day and skipped happy hour. It wasn't adding value to my life, and it cost me dearly. It was an awakening. I redirected my thoughts to saving and investing money. Our income increased and our stress decreased. It was a total game-changer.

43. Finish!

We rarely achieve our goals because we follow a dysfunctional process. January 1st comes, and we are excited. We have 20+ goals. We get a health club membership and complete our business plan. Our willpower is at an all-time high because this is the year everything changes.

We start strong, but we can't find our plan by February. We can't find the health club, and no one else can either. We believe we have plenty of time to hit our goals. There is no urgency, and we drift.

The middle of the year arrives, and we still think there is time. September comes, and we finally look at our goals. "No way that will happen; we will start anew on January 1st." We give up and drift the rest of the year.

We then repeat this flawed process. Nothing changes and we remain stuck. Why doesn't this work? We have too many goals and too much time.

To get better results do the following: Pick your most important goal. Take the annual goal and break it down. Focus on the first 90 days. Where do you need to be by March 31st to be on target?

Break it down further to a weekly goal. This creates focus and urgency. Develop the weekly plan. At the end of the week, assess the results. Ask yourself what worked and what didn't? Make small changes for the next week.

Most importantly, finish each week and quarter. Run all the way through the tape, regardless of how far you're behind. Become a finisher. You might not hit the goal when you want, but you will eventually if you don't quit.

Quote: "Starting strong is good. Finishing strong is epic." – Robin Sharma, Author, Speaker.

Resource: *The 12-week year*, by Brian Moran

Action Step: Journal:

1. Pick your #1 goal.
2. Where do you need to be at the end of this quarter?
3. What is the weekly goal for which to aim?
4. Create your plan to hit the weekly mark.
5. Get moving and have fun.

I was a great goal-setter but a horrible goal-achiever. I loved the feeling of the new year with renewed hope and possibilities. I enjoyed making my annual plan. I spent many hours and set many goals. Unfortunately, my plan was long and complex, and the process didn't work. I stayed stuck for many years. I would forget what I committed to and drift. There was no urgency, and I never finished.

I learned a better way. January 1st arrived. With my back against the wall, I needed to do something different. We needed to double our income and eliminate debt to reach financial breakeven. It seemed impossible. I took the annual income goal and focused on the first quarter ending March 31st. To track, I had to hit 25% of the annual goal. It still seemed big but more doable.

I developed a simple weekly plan to hit the weekly income goal that aligned with the 90-day goal. I had achieved that weekly goal before, so my belief increased. On Saturdays, I recorded the weekly income generated and assessed the plan. I made a few small weekly course corrections. This was easier than making 20+ changes all at once.

March 31st arrived, and I hit 52% of the goal. I fell way short, but my confidence increased. I kept my word and ran to the end of the quarter. I finished for the first time ever. In the past, I would've called this failure and beat myself up. I would've reduced or changed the goal, but not this time. Instead, I called it progress, and I was learning.

I reset the same goal. I hit 74% of the goal in Q2, so I re-upped again. Finally, I hit 88% of it in Q3. For Q4, I raised the income goal. Every time I got close to hitting the quarterly goal, I would raise the target.

We've set goals this way for 52 quarters and have only hit the income goal twice. We've missed it 96% of the time, but our income is five times higher. We use this strategy for all our goals. It's simple and creates focus. It spurs growth and forces me to finish.

Pillar 5

The Dream

44. Know What You Want and Focus On It!

If we're specific, we can have anything we want. The masses are vague. It's more of a wish. People don't know what they want, and it's a convenient cop-out. If we stay in confusion, we never have to commit. It's an excuse for not moving forward and a trap for mediocrity. We live in fear and hide. We focus on what we don't want.

The mind is powerful and finds evidence to support our behavior. We overcome one problem after another, which is exhausting. To shift, we must think. We must shift our focus from problems to goals.

It's work to change decades of habitual thought patterns. If we persist, we cross the magical threshold where most of our thoughts are positive. It's an amazing feeling.

Review what you want every morning; it helps entrench new thinking. Our minds are rigged for distraction, and high performers place reminders everywhere. Pictures of their goals on the bathroom mirror, phone, car, and office. They never leave success to chance. We need constant reminders of our commitments.

During the day, collect evidence that you're on the right path. Celebrate small wins. It increases your energy and focus. What you focus on eventually materializes.

Quote: "Nothing is more necessary for success as the single-minded pursuit of an objective." – Fred Smith, Founder of FedEx

Resource: *The Magic of Thinking Big* by David J. Schwartz, PH.D.

Action Step: Journal:

1. Write down what you want.
2. If you don't know, write down everything you don't want.
3. The opposite of the don't list will get you clear on what you do want.
4. List multiple reasons for each item.
5. Look at it every day.
6. Set up reminders in different locations to keep focus.

I've been blessed with world-class mentoring, but initially, I ignored it. I was constantly looking for the secret. I would receive instruction, take notes, and continue my search. Surely, what I just learned wasn't the secret.

Every mentor had a consistent message. First, you must be clear on what you want. Focus on it, don't focus on problems and obstacles. Great point: I would write that down. Note to self – "Chris, get clear; very important." Then I would close my notebook and do nothing. At the next training, a different coach would repeat the same "get clear" principle. I would repeat the process yet never gain clarity.

My coaches always asked what I was aiming for? What did I really want? Like the masses, I was vague, and my answers were more about impressing them. I wanted more money, a larger business, etc. But when pressed for specifics, I would stumble, stammer, and hesitate, which was a sure sign of confusion.

I was in a leadership meeting discussing the how-tos and details of our business. One of the top mentors arrived halfway through and heard the discussion. His face said it all. He noisily interrupted the meeting and said, "I don't know what you all are talking about. This isn't that important. If you don't know where you're going, this is useless. From the beginning, I have always known what I want, and most importantly, I know why. That's why I'm smoking all of you. I can communicate what I want and why I want it in a few seconds. You all have no clue. So instead of getting clear, you mess around with this stuff." Then he left the room.

It finally registered. He started in our business two years after me, yet he was way ahead. I resolved to get this handled. I defined financial freedom and set my goals. Most importantly, I connected to why it mattered.

I looked at it every morning. I visualized, affirmed, and posted reminders everywhere. Fast forward a few months later. At breakfast, my mentor asked what I was aiming for. Within one minute, I listed the metrics I was chasing and my top reasons. I was clear and spoke with conviction. I was confident and certain, with no hesitation. He said, "Chris, there is no doubt you will hit what you just told me."

He was right; we nailed it. I've coached many people on the necessity of clarity. Most do what I previously did. They are vague and stay stuck in the how-tos and details.

I always know when someone is about to hit their goal. I have the same feeling as my coach did. They are clear with conviction in their voice. It rarely happens. The others hesitate, are vague and typically stay stuck. They focus on drama and issues. They discuss problems instead of their vision. They don't know what they want. They take notes on clarity and never do anything about it.

Don't fall into this trap. Get clear and keep it front and center.

45. Know the Feeling You Want

Our actions are driven by a feeling we want to experience. Our subconscious mind is powerful, and we must feed it with the right material for the best results. It understands feelings, not words. When we impress the subconscious with emotions, it filters our environment. It alerts us to what's necessary to hit our goal.

The best description of the subconscious mind is given by Emmet Fox in *Around the Year*. "As soon as our subconscious mind accepts any idea, it goes to work. It uses every bit of knowledge we've ever collected to achieve its purpose. It mobilizes our mental powers, most of which we've never consciously used. It lines up the laws of nature as they operate both inside and outside of us, to get its way."

He continues. "Sometimes it succeeds immediately. Other times it takes a while. If the goal is not utterly impossible, the subconscious succeeds. The law is true for both good and bad ideas. When used negatively, it brings sickness, trouble, and failure. When used positively, it brings healing, freedom, and success. We give the orders, and the subconscious does the work."

The orders represent clearly identifying the feeling we want to experience. Much like an untended garden, the weeds of negativity grow naturally. We weed the garden by planting the seeds of positive feelings.

Quote: "The first secret of getting what you want is knowing what you want." – Arthur D. Hlavaty, Writer, and Publisher

Resource: *The Feeling is the Secret* by Neville Goddard

Action Step: Visualize your #1 goal as already accomplished. Before you begin visualizing, identify the feeling you want. It's imperative you feel it when visualizing your desired result.

As a CPA, I lived mainly in my head. The discussion of feelings went against my belief that brains win the day. Discussing how I felt was uncomfortable, and my thinking was, "Let's not go there." I was living from my head, not my heart. It was easier to repress my emotions.

I was a human doing, not a human being. It worked in a job, but not in real life. As my personal development journey progressed, I thought about past successes. The feeling of pride was my driver. I wanted to be acknowledged. I wanted people to be proud of me. I learned I could be more intentional with my goals and desires, and the feeling was the secret.

Impressing my subconscious mind with the feeling I wanted helped unlock the power. I was stuck and had to do everything possible to avoid failure. This included never missing my morning visualization session.

Visualizing what I wanted for a few minutes a day was the habit. I was coached to visualize with emotion and feeling. This was a struggle, as I usually just went through the motions. Let's be done with it and check it off my list. More human doing behavior.

The breakthrough was identifying the feeling I wanted before starting my visualization session. The feeling I wanted was financial relief, and I needed it like oxygen. I was sick of the stress, and I wanted relief. I focused on this feeling; I stopped the negative, and my sessions went to the next level. I imagined my ideal scene and felt it deeply. The seed was planted, and the desire was created.

We started getting ahead financially. We could finally save money. I remember waking at 3 a.m. and sitting up in bed. This happened for many years and was usually triggered by fear and anxiety. This time was different; I felt relief. I connected it back to my visualization sessions.

It was one of the greatest feelings in my life. The money was great, but the feeling was infinitely better. Things were never the same again.

46. Affirm What You Want

Affirmations are statements we repeat to shift our mindset. They help us feel better and raise our self-esteem. They reprogram our beliefs and transform our results. Positive thoughts manifest positive results. The more we repeat the positive, the more they become ingrained.

There are opposing views on affirmations. One group believes they work, and the other thinks they're useless. They're both correct because whatever you believe becomes your experience. The results in your life will be determined by what you repeatedly tell yourself and the images you hold in your mind.

We are always affirming, whether it be positive or negative. It takes work to shift from negative to positive, but it's worth it. The life you want hinges on this strategy.

Quote: "Whatever you choose to believe comes true for you. You can change your life by changing your thoughts." – Louise Hay, Author, Speaker, and Founder of Hay House.

Resource: *You Can Heal Your Life* by Louise Hay

Action Step: Based on your #1 Goal, list 2-3 affirmations you can read and recite.

The Keys
- Written in the first person.
- Positive, not negative (example: I am healthy vs. I am not fat)
- Emotional charge. What feeling do you want?
- Present Tense (I am, not I will).

Affirmations transformed my life, yet initially, I didn't believe they worked. My logical CPA brain dismissed the concept. I unknowingly used negative affirmations to create limiting results. I attracted what I mentally affirmed. I told myself I was not good enough, not deserving, and wealth was for others. Life was all about overcoming challenges, stress, and struggle. I believed that life was a bitch, and then you die.

With nothing to lose, I started applying positive affirmations. It wasn't a quick fix. It required time and focus. However, I began to see the outside world match my inner dialogue. The affirmation that energized me the most was:

"I attract success, abundance & peace into my life because that is who I am."

I said this a thousand times, often when there was no evidence. Yet things started to change, and we began experiencing financial success. We bought a second home in Keystone, Colorado, on a small lake. We loved it. I enjoyed running along the Snake River.

I imagined and affirmed this condo. I dreamed of my kids sleeping in bunk beds during their summer visit. I visualized being with my family and having a blast in the mountains. All of this came true. What I affirmed eventually happened.

Coming back from a run, a thought hit me like a lightning bolt. I stopped; the affirmation had become true. I was THAT. I was success, abundance and peace. I no longer needed to affirm these things; I was living them. Tears rushed down my face. I stood silent, realizing the work had been worth it. Affirming these things brought them into my life.

47. Hold The Image

To succeed, we must know what we want and why. Without focus, we risk settling for whatever life hands us. We become the proverbial beach ball being tossed around randomly on the waves of life. What we think about, we bring about.

The outside-in approach allows our thinking to be dictated by our environment. Without thought intervention, our feelings are subject to outside circumstances, both good and bad. This emotional roller coaster creates stress and tension. To achieve different results, we must think differently.

The inside-out approach yields better results. Our outcomes are based on the images we hold in our minds and what we repeatedly tell ourselves. High performers create an image of success and work towards its development. Whether or not they see immediate results, successful people trust the process. They believe everything happens for a reason, as they persist in holding tight to their dreams.

Quote: "Keep your mind on a higher image rather than a lower concern. I realize that is not always an easy thing to do, but it sure pays great dividends for the person who develops the mental strength to do it, and that is what it takes-mental strength." – Philip Nicola, Minister.

Resource: Read Chapter 3, The Image Maker, of You Were Born Rich by Bob Proctor.

Action Step:
- Close your eyes and relax.
- Think of something you really want.
- Play a mental movie of what achieving that goal would mean.
- What would it feel like to achieve this?
- Identify the feelings (relief, joy, happiness).
- Really feel it.
- Visualize 3 to 5 minutes per day.
- You are planting seeds in fertile soil.
- Stick with it.

During my darkest days, I visualized my dreams coming true. I saw myself onstage at our company convention, being recognized in front of 30,000 people. This scene created tears of joy and symbolized the end of stress and struggle. I repeated this visualization thousands of times and experienced a sense of elation. Then I would awaken to my lackluster reality.

I'd hear my coach's voice in my head telling me that it requires more than hard work; it's the mental toughness to hold the desired image minus the need for external affirmation.

This advice was difficult to trust, but I had no options. My back was against the wall. What didn't work was my habit of dreaming, followed by depression from my current results. However, I eventually developed the necessary mental strength. Years later, I was asked to serve as an emcee at our company's national convention.

In my 10-minute opening, I shared the story of deciding to recommit to my business and succeed. How I had to tell my kids, when they were little, that I wouldn't see them for a while. I showed the audience a photograph of that day and then brought my son Caden, now age 18, onstage. The crowd went crazy. On my 48th birthday, my dream became a reality.

Later, my team threw a birthday party at the Waldorf Hotel. I sat in a chair for two hours while each person stated how I had impacted their life. It was an amazing experience to also hear my wife and son share their feelings. So often, we're not aware of our impact.

It was a life-changing experience and confirmation that what you think about comes about. It proved that a picture in the mind can become a reality.

48. Get Wealthy

Money is one of the most emotional topics. Our parents, people of influence, and society programmed us to believe that money is bad. Money is the second most mentioned topic in the Bible.

The media, movies, and television portray wealthy people in a negative light. Society believes they are miserable, back-stabbing, horrible people. The masses fear they will become these people if they get wealthy.

Exposure to these messages creates a belief that wealth is bad. As a result, we block our wealth and miss opportunities. We don't ask, follow up, or follow through. We procrastinate and hesitate.

Being broke creates stress for us and our families. The mind virus can perpetuate for generations, eventually impacting our health and relationships. Financial stress is deadly.

Money is a neutral topic; what we add to it is our experience. Like a hammer, it can be used for good or bad. Money makes a great person better and a bad person worse. Just like oxygen, we need it.

Intently study this subject. We are storytellers. The results in our lives are directly tied to the stories we create. Uncover your money story and assess the price for you and your family. Change and upgrade your story. Find positive reasons for becoming wealthy. How will it positively impact you and your family? Who could you help?

Peace of mind is difficult to obtain without money. Resolve to become wealthy.

Quote: "If a person gets his attitude toward money straight, it will help straighten out almost every other area of his life." – Billy Graham, American Evangelist

Resource: *How Rich People Think* by Steve Siebold

Action Step: Get a Money Journal.

1. First step – Write the word "money."
2. List everything you make up about that word.
3. Write an empowering story that attracts wealth.
4. Review often and assess your progress.

I committed to changing my relationship with money. How could a CPA and Financial Advisor be broke? I knew what to do, but I wasn't doing it. How was my thinking creating financial lack?

I purchased a green journal and wrote "money" at the top of the first page. What did that word mean to me? What stories was I making up about it? I was a great storyteller. If I could shift the story, I could change the results. It became apparent why I was broke; my thinking was broken. It was a long list of bad stories blocking my wealth.

- Rich people are crooks.
- Money is made on the backs of poor people.
- Money, you either have it, or you don't.
- I don't deserve money.
- Can have fun or money but never both.
- Money will never make me happy.
- I had guilt for being wealthy while others suffered.

What a game-changing exercise. Why didn't I do this before? How could I go decades and never inventory the thoughts that created so much stress? I was grateful that I finally did. I wrote out the new story I wanted.

- Money is Good.
- Money is a scorecard of the value I bring to others.
- If I'm growing, so is my money.
- Making and saving big money is easy.
- I'm a good person, and money will make me better.
- I attract success, abundance, and peace into my life because that is who I am.
- I deserve to be wealthy.

I intently focused on these affirmations with emotion and feeling. It was time to control my thoughts. Anytime I would begin to drift to the old story, I would smile, laugh, and redirect. It wasn't overnight, but eventually, everything changed.

49. You Can Do It

Success is possible, but we must focus on areas that increase the odds. It's an inside game as our beliefs determine our results. We must do the work to upgrade our beliefs. It takes effort to change and that scares people. Instead, the masses create excuses for why they can't do it.

Most people don't pay attention to their associations. Their peer group has similar success and beliefs. They confirm and condone each other's level of success. The group doesn't want the others to grow. Crab mentality takes over. Just as one is ready to leave the bucket, another pulls them back down. The "If I can't have it, neither can you" mentality keeps everyone stuck.

They believe more successful people possess something they don't. Others are smarter, a certain color, background, male/female. This leads to a miserable existence. Don't fall for it.

To reverse this, you must have a personal development plan. You must work on yourself. Pick one limiting belief to upgrade; read and listen to everything you can. Apply what you've learned. It's a project, not a problem. You will eventually change.

You must associate with the right people and connect with those living your desired results. Connect with leaders who inspire you to upgrade your thoughts and actions. Prune others in your life.

Most people aren't burned out but drained out. Their energy is zapped by the battery drainers. Most people have heard that our associations are crucial, but they do nothing about it.

Lastly, delayed gratification is mandatory. If you are inclined to seek instant gratification, success will elude you. We must give up all that interferes with our main goal. Self-denial is more difficult than hard work.

We must never sacrifice our spirituality, family, or health. If those are compromised for the attainment of the desire, it's a loss, not a win. The result does not justify the price.

Get excited about the process. Get excited about the people you will help and the life you will create. Imagine what it will feel like. Others have done it and so can you.

Quote: "Whether you think you can or think you can't you're right." – Henry Ford, American Industrialist

Resource: *The Happiness Advantage* by Shawn Achor

Action Step: Journal:

1. Who are the top three associations in your life?
2. Is this the group that will get you to the next level?
3. If not, upgrade your associations.
4. Reach out to five people who you admire.
5. Interview them on what makes them successful.

I started my entrepreneurial journey with many negatives. I resigned from my job with five weeks of savings, and the security of my salary was gone. I had only made $8,000 in my business the prior 12 months, part-time. I successfully spent the first year talking people out of doing business with me. I wasn't very good.

I had no office. Home base was an 800-square-foot condo in Central Denver. I was leaving the crab bucket, and many tried pulling me back down. They thought I was stupid and throwing away a promising career. They all swore I would be back. They told others at my firm to not follow me. I felt like the whole world was against me. I was afraid, but I had some things on my side.

I ignored advice from people who weren't living the life I wanted. This was ingrained early. So, the naysayers had no impact on me.

My associations changed, and I stayed connected to those in my corner. They cheered me on, and I let the rest go. One of my best friends let me share an office with him. He was a huge encourager and a great business partner. I am forever grateful that he stepped up.

Every Monday morning, my business partners and I met for strict accountability. I mostly disliked that meeting, but I would've quit without it. They knew I needed accountability. It was all about results. We reported what we did and what we needed to change. The first order of business was to stay in business.

We were coachable and got mentored by those who were where we wanted to be. The world-class mentoring I've received throughout my career has been a major blessing. I would be nothing without these associations. I'm so grateful for their mentorship.

My desire was proving I could do it and proving others wrong. Anytime I felt adversity and doubted myself, I would imagine quitting and running into a hater. The thought of telling them that I quit made me sick. I instantly shook off the negative and moved forward. The naysayers were an asset. Without them, who knows where I would be. They were a blessing, although I didn't recognize it until later.

I had a delayed gratification muscle. I didn't need instant results. The vision of a better life kept moving me forward. I knew the wait would be worth it.

If someone else could do it, I could too. It wasn't could I, but would I? Would I do the work necessary? I just needed time and effort to compound.

I worked on myself and took action. That combination transformed my beliefs and results.

Last and most important. I'm forever grateful to those who trusted and believed in me. My family, teammates, clients, friends, and acquaintances. It takes a team to make anything happen. We can't do it on our own. I'm nothing without all these amazing people. I had a lot of people step up and help me. I am blessed. I love these people, and I'm forever grateful.

These aren't all the ingredients to our success. But without this foundation, it would've been impossible. I am blessed beyond belief. If I can succeed, then you certainly can too.

50. It's Worth It

Is it going to be worth it?

Will the work and sacrifice lead to success?

What if it doesn't work out?

Everyone has doubts and fears. The quitters don't believe in themselves and expect failure. They want the easy route and don't believe the effort will be worth it. Unfortunately, this group can't be helped or coached.

Another group barely tries; they are interested in success but not committed. They give partial effort and never fully engage. They have a plan B, a chicken exit. Their mindset is, "If this doesn't work out, then I'll go do this." They lack conviction and verbalize their doubts to others. They fail, pick up, and go somewhere else. The cycle repeats.

The third group is the achievers. They understand that success comes in stages. Initially, we aren't that good, and few people are naturals. When things come easily, we often bail when it gets tough. Don't wish it were easy.

We were all initially bad at learning to walk or drive a car. The achievers know and accept this. They go all in acquiring the skills and mentality necessary to succeed. They don't suffer from the "will it work?" mind virus of the masses. They don't hope it will work; they expect it to.

They still have doubts and fears but take action to overcome them. Successful people aren't concerned with when. They operate from "until." They work until it happens. They understand that if you can't succeed where you are, taking your old self into a new opportunity won't magically create success. Figure it out where you are.

It might take years or decades. They want success sooner, but persist knowing it will be worth it. Mostly, they fear regret. They don't want their golden years consumed with remorse. Their fear of regret outweighs their fear of failure, and it's the gas that keeps them moving.

Quote: "Will it be easy? No. Will it be worth it? Absolutely." – Unknown

Resource: *The Ed Mylett Podcast*, The Real AF Podcast

Action Step: Assess what camp you're in:

1. Quitter
2. Chicken Exit
3. Until.

If not in #3, what change needs to happen to be a 3?

Starting in college, I asked successful people if it was worth it. They were never confused by the question. Without hesitation, they all said it was. I collected evidence that the effort would be worth it. I never questioned it.

I wasn't naturally talented. I had many deficits to overcome. I did the work and development to counteract these deficiencies. I've been mindful of the "it's worth it" rewards along the way.

Whether it be a win for my family or a person I helped. I remind myself that the work was and will continue to be worth it. I'm human, like everyone else, with a bias toward comfort. These reminders fuel the work that I continue to do. I have many "it's worth it" stories, but this is a favorite:

I'm grateful that I made the changes to stay in my kids' lives. I live in Colorado, and they live in Atlanta. I'd made more than 100 trips to see them. These visits helped keep our relationship strong. Both are brilliant kids, and we'll chalk that up to mom's side of the family. Their mom has done an amazing, world-class job raising them. Their stepdad is a star as well.

The fall of Caden's senior year was college application time. He applied to 12 colleges, but Vanderbilt was his #1 choice, a top 15 school in the nation. Being apart, I missed many moments, but I was fortunate to witness many memorable sports and school events. This moment was the top.

We were at Carson's basketball game in mid-December. At any moment, Caden would be notified of Vanderbilt's decision. He finally gets the email that he was accepted. Some poor kid was shooting a free throw when I screamed at the top of my lungs and freaked everyone out. He was in.

Their mom stood at the door of the gym in tears. A major validation that her hard work paid off. I ran over and gave her a hug.

I said, "Good for you." Her response was, "No, good for us!" I get emotional every time I think about her comment.

She was right. Moments like these are miracles. The past struggles, failures, arguments, and pain instantly vanished. I forgot all of it. I thanked God for the blessing and our family for persisting. Anything I/we ever went through was worth that moment. The emotion is still there like it was yesterday; I will never forget it.

Conclusion

I trust this book has been transformative and valuable for you. I thoroughly enjoyed writing it and never lost my enthusiasm during the process. I was excited to share these ideas and concepts that were so life-changing for me.

Growth and personal development are an infinite game. We will never be done growing as there are always new levels to achieve.

If you're just beginning, this might not sound like good news. However, once you start, create momentum, and see the results, you'll realize that the effort is more than worth it.

The best part about growing is the difference we make in others' lives. The lifestyle of growth and development takes discipline. Sometimes, our ego attempts to convince us that the effort isn't worth it.

However, for years I've taken note of the difference it has made for others. Whether it was coaching, speaking, or a share on social media, people have articulated the impact.

You never know when something small can significantly change someone's world.

I've collected much evidence of the impact and know that the focus, effort, and discipline are worth it. The ripple effect is everlasting.

Thank you for reading and allowing me to contribute to your life. This has furthered my dream and purpose of helping others free themselves mentally so they can live amazing lives.

I hope this serves you to create the extraordinary life that you deserve. I pray for success, peace, and fulfillment for you and your family. God Bless.

Acknowledgements

This book is made possible only because of the people who loved and supported me. I'm grateful for all those who have poured into me over the years. It takes a large team for any individual to succeed and I've been blessed to have been coached, helped, and guided by many world class individuals. There are way too many people to list for fear of leaving someone out.

I'm grateful for my mom, her selfless love and care, and all the amazing values she instilled in me. I'm thankful for my Dad for his teachings and the lessons I learned. I am grateful for my family and their love and support.

Thank you to the coaches and mentors who invested countless hours and believed in me when I often did not believe in myself. I am forever grateful that you saw things in me well before I did. I am eternally grateful for your love, care, wisdom, and guidance.

I thank our amazing entrepreneurial business platform and our incredible team and clients. Our success only happens with our world-class team and loyal clients. Their love and support are appreciated as they stood by my side through the good and bad.

To my world-class wife, Marlow, without you, I'm lost. None of our success happens without you. I thank God for you every day.

To my incredible kids, Caden & Carson, you are my inspiration, and I always want to make you proud of your Dad. I am so proud of you, and it's an incredible blessing to watch your kids be way better than you.

I thank Steve Siebold for all your coaching and teaching over the years. I'm grateful for your coaching on this book. I appreciate your insight, care, and diligence in helping my dream come true.

None of this would be possible without my Heavenly Father and Savior, Jesus Christ. Thanks for never giving up on me. The peace I experience would've forever escaped me. I'm grateful that God's Hand has and will continue to guide me.

Chris Felton
Matthew 6:33

BE WILLING TO CHANGE.
DO THE WORK.
IT'S WORTH IT!!

Get the Think & Grow You Bonus Bundle

Visit www.chrisfelton.me/book/bookbonuses to get access to Chris Felton's Think & Grow You bonus bundle.

Tap into Chris' thoughts, actions, and strategies that will change your life forever, including:

- ➤ Printable PDF book of Think & Grow You quotes
- ➤ Printable PDF book of Think & Grow You resources
- ➤ Printable PDF book of The Quotable Chris Felton
- ➤ Printable PDF book of Think & Grow You action steps, including journaling space to complete each action step
- ➤ Exclusive content with Chris
- ➤ Access to all of Chris' social media channels

About the Author

Chris Felton is a bestselling author and ultra-successful entrepreneur. Over his 23-year career, Chris leads a national team of advisors that have helped over 17,000 clients. He's achieved Top 1% status in a company of 50,000+ agents. As a thought leader in the financial services industry, Chris' insights have been featured in major media outlets such as US News & World Report, Market Watch, Yahoo Finance, and Nasdaq to name a few.

As an international speaker and bestselling author, Chris is committed to sharing his story and lessons learned from being on the brink of financial ruin and divorce to building one of the most successful financial services firms in the country. He speaks on stages to audiences of over 20,000 and appears on top podcasts, such as the Ed Mylett show, reaching millions of listeners around the world.

While he's achieved a lot of business success, life is about more than money for Chris. He supports causes focused on eradicating poverty, animal rescue shelters, and his company's foundation that focuses on supporting local charities for its agents.

With his latest book and speaking series "Think and Grow You", Chris is focused on helping people break through plateaus in their growth by learning how to get out of their own way and take their success, peace, and impact to the next level.

www.thinkgrowyou.com
www.chrisfelton.me

CPSIA information can be obtained
at www.ICGtesting.com
Printed in the USA
JSHW031212260223
38183JS00005B/13

9 781666 400182